ON JOB

GUSTAVO GUTIÉRREZ

ON JOB

God-Talk and the Suffering
of the Innocent

Translated from the Spanish by
Matthew J. O'Connell

ORBIS BOOKS

Maryknoll, New York 10545

Second Printing, January 1988

The Catholic Foreign Mission Society of America (Maryknoll) recruits and trains people for overseas missionary service. Through Orbis Books Maryknoll aims to foster the international dialogue that is essential to mission. The books published, however, reflect the opinions of their authors and are not meant to represent the official position of the society.

Originally published as *Hablar de Dios desde el sufrimiento del inocente* by Centro de Estudios y Publicaciones, 1986, Lima, Peru, and Instituto Bartolomé de Las Casas, Lima-Rímae, Peru
© 1985 by Instituto Bartolomé de Las Casas

English translation copyright © 1987 by Orbis Books, Maryknoll, NY 10545

Manuscript Editor: William E. Jerman

Unless otherwise indicated, Bible quotations for the Book of Job are from *The New Jerusalem Bible,* copyright © 1985 by Darton, Longman & Todd, Ltd. and Doubleday & Company, Inc. Reprinted by permission of the publisher. The *Revised Standard Version* has been used for the other books of the Bible.

Library of Congress Cataloging-in-Publication Data
Gutiérrez, Gustavo, 1928-
  On Job.
  Translation of: Hablar de Dios desde el sufrimiento
del inocente.
  Includes index.
  1. Bible.   O.T.   Job—Criticism, interpretation, etc.
2. Suffering—Biblical teaching.   3. Liberation theology.
I. Title.   II. Title: God-talk and the suffering of the
innocent.
BS1415.2.G8813   1987   223'.106   87-5661
ISBN 0-88344-577-8
ISBN 0-88344-552-2 (pbk.)

To my parents,
who were the first to speak of God to me,
I dedicate these pages written
in seasons of suffering and hope.

To the people of Ayacucho who,
like Job,
suffer unjustly and cry out
to the God of life.

My mother told me:
If you stone the white fledglings,
God will punish you;
if you hit your friend,
the boy with the donkey face,
God will punish you.

It was God's sign
of the two sticks;*
and the commandments of God
fitted into my hands
like ten more fingers.

Today they tell me:
If you do not love war,
if you do not kill a dove a day,
God will punish you;
if you do not strike the black,
if you do not hate the Amerindian,
God will punish you;
if you give the poor ideas
instead of a kiss,
if you talk to them of justice
instead of charity,
God will punish you,
God will punish you.

Mamma, is that really
our God?

    Juan Gonzalo Rose, *La Pregunta*

*A reference to the cross.

Contents

Introduction

Theology is talk about God. According to the Bible, however, God is a mystery, and at the beginning of his *Summa Theologiae* Thomas Aquinas states as a basic principle governing all theological reflection that "we cannot know what God is but only what God is not."[1] Must we not think, then, that theology sets itself an impossible task?

No, the task is not impossible. But it is important to keep in mind from the very outset that theological thought about God is *thought about a mystery.* I mention this here because it influences an attitude to be adopted in the effort to talk about God. I mean an attitude of respect that is incompatible with the kind of God-talk that is sure, at times arrogantly sure, that it knows everything there is to know about God. José María Arguedas poses the question: "Is not what we know far less than the great hope we feel?"[2] This question will bring an unhesitating, humble yes from those who believe in the God of Jesus Christ.

Let me make it clear, however, that when we talk of "mystery" with the Bible in mind, we do not mean something that is hidden and *must remain* hidden. The "mystery" in this case must rather be expressed, not concealed; communicated, not kept to itself. E. Jüngel puts it well: in the Christian perspective, "the fact of having to be revealed belongs to the essence of mystery."[3] According to Paul, revelation in this case is "the revelation of the mystery which was kept secret for long ages but is now disclosed and through the prophetic writings is made known to all nations, according to the command of the eternal God, to bring about the obedience of faith" (Rom. 16:25–26). The revelation of the mystery of God leads to its proclamation to every human being: this is the special characteristic of the biblical message regarding mystery. Reflection on the mystery of God must therefore begin with God's resolve of self-communication to "all nations" (Matt. 28:19). The setting and requirements of the proclamation are fundamental presuppositions of any theologizing.

REVELATION AND THEOLOGICAL METHOD

The point I have just made leads me to discuss two connections as I begin these pages on talk about God.

1. The first is the relationship between *revelation* and *gratuitousness.* Christ reveals that the Father who sent him on a universal mission is a God of love. This revelation assigns a privileged place to the simple and the despised, as Jesus made clear: "I thank thee, Father, Lord of heaven and earth, that thou

hast hidden these things from the wise and understanding and revealed them to babes; yea, Father, for such was thy gracious will" (Matt. 11:25–26).

The words "wise and understanding" refer to a social and religious minority in Israel: the teachers, or doctors, of the law, the high priests, and the scribes. These were the men who sat "on the chair of Moses" (Matt. 23:2) and had taken possession of "the key of knowledge" (Luke 11:52). They were the ones who attributed the works of Jesus to the power of Beelzebul (see Matt. 12:24). They were important and religious persons. When Jesus said that the revelation given by the Father was hidden from the teachers, he was directly opposing the accepted and usual view of his day. He was challenging the religious and social authority of the experts in the law and saying that, because of the Father's predilection for them, the ignorant had a greater capacity for understanding revelation. This statement is one more sign of the originality of Jesus' teaching. He was here attacking the very foundation of the religious world of his time—namely, the identification of the primary addressees of God's word.

Over against the wise and understanding are the "babes." The Greek word Matthew uses here (*nēpioi*—literally, "very young children") carries a clear connotation of ignorance. This is the point of the contrast with the "wise and understanding." Scholars agree that *nēpioi* here does not refer to moral or spiritual dispositions; rather the word has a certain pejorative overtone. The *nēpioi* in this context are the ignorant, those who must be led along the right path because they do not know how to guide themselves.[4]

The "little children" are related to the poor, the hungry, and the afflicted (Luke 6:20–23); to sinners and the sick (who are despised on this account) (Matt. 9:12–13); to sheep who have no shepherd (Matt. 9:36); to the little ones (Matt. 10:42; 18:1–4); to those not invited to the banquet (Luke 14:16–24). All these categories form a bloc, a sector of the people; they are "the poor of the land."

The ignorance in question is not in itself a virtue or a merit that explains the divine preference. What we see here is simply a situation of need. By the same token, wisdom is not a demerit or something that provokes divine rejection. The "wise" are not necessarily proud in the moral sense; they may be, and indeed that is a danger for them. So too the ignorant may be humble, but they are not always such; humility is simply a possibility for them. It follows that the condition of being privileged addressees of revelation is the result not primarily of moral or spiritual dispositions but of a human situation in which God undertakes self-revelation by acting and overturning values and criteria. The scorned of this world are those whom the God of love prefers. This is a very simple matter, but for a mind that judges everything by merits and demerits, worthiness and unworthiness, it is difficult to grasp.

It must be said, however, that the reason for Jesus' gratitude is not primarily, as might appear, the fact that revelation has been hidden from some and granted to others. The structure of the sentence might suggest this interpretation, but the interpretation is wrong, as can be shown by a comparison with other passages that, like this one, use contrast in a distinctively Semitic way to emphasize a point. The fact that God hides "these things" from the wise and reveals them to the simple is the concrete occasion for grasping what is behind this behavior and gives it its meaning—namely, *the free and unmerited love of God* for every human being and especially for the poor and forgotten. This interpretation of Jesus' words is supported by the undeniable fact that the gospel treats this truth as a key element in the message of Jesus.

The real reason, then, for Jesus' gratitude is his contemplation (in the full sense of the term as a form of prayer) of the Father's goodness and love that reach out to the simple and the unimportant, and give them preference. This predilection, which does not imply exclusivity, is underscored by the hiding of revelation from the wise and important. An entire social and religious order is hereby turned upside down.

The dominant element in the text as a whole is the gratuitous character of God's love. Puebla puts the matter very clearly:

> The poor merit preferential attention, whatever may be the moral or spiritual situation in which they find themselves. Made in the image and likeness of God to be his children, this image is dimmed and even defiled. That is why God takes on their defense and loves them [§1142].[5]

The ultimate basis of God's preference for the poor is to be found in God's own goodness and not in any analysis of society or in human compassion, however pertinent these reasons may be.

2. The second connection has to do with *the way or method of speaking about God.* The text I cited from St. Thomas at the beginning of this Introduction tells us of the limits or, if you prefer, the proper place of theological reflection. In defining the work of theology, this brings us to a theme that is central both to classic theology and to theology of liberation.[6]

The point I want to make can be stated thus: God is first contemplated when we do God's will and allow God to reign; only after that do we think about God. To use familiar categories: contemplation and practice together make up a *first act*; theologizing is a *second act.*[7] We must first establish ourselves on the terrain of spirituality and practice; only subsequently is it possible to formulate discourse on God in an authentic and respectful way. Theologizing done without the mediation of contemplation and practice does not meet the requirements of the God of the Bible. The mystery of God comes to life in contemplation and in the practice of God's plan for human history; only in a second phase can this life inspire appropriate reasoning and relevant speech. (Given the two meanings of the Greek word *logos*—"reason" and "word"— theology is a reasoned word or reason put into words.) In view of all this we can say that the first stage is *silence,* the second is *speech.*

Contemplation and practice feed each other; the two together make up the stage of silence before God. In prayer we remain speechless, we simply place ourselves before the Lord. To a degree, we remain silent in our practice as well, for in our involvements, in our daily work, we do not talk about God all the time; we do indeed live in God, but not by discoursing on God. As Ecclesiastes says, "there is a time to keep silence, and a time to speak" (3:7b). Silence, the time of quiet, is first act and the necessary mediation for the time of speaking about the Lord or doing theo-logy, which is second act.

The time of silence is the time of loving encounter with God and of prayer and commitment; it is a time of "staying with him" (John 1:39). As the experience of human love shows us, in this kind of encounter we enter depths and regions that are ineffable. When words do not suffice, when they are incapable of communicating what is experienced at the affective level, then we are fully engaged in loving. And when words are incapable of showing forth our experience, we fall back on symbols, which are another way of remaining silent. For when we use a symbol, we do not speak; we let an object or gesture speak for us. This is precisely how we proceed in the liturgy; symbolic language is the language of a love that transcends words.

This is why images of human love are so often used in the Bible in speaking of the relations between God and the people of God. When two lovers fall silent and simply remain in each other's presence, they know that they are experiencing love of each other at a deeper level. Silence, contemplation, and practice are all necessary mediations in thinking about God and doing theology. Theology will then be speech that has been enriched by silence. This reflective discourse will in turn feed the silence of contemplation and practice, and give it new dimensions.

Gratuitousness and revelation, silence and speech: these are two presuppositions of the effort at understanding our faith. I shall be keeping them in mind in the following pages in which I raise a question about God that emerges out of our experience in Latin America as we share the life and faith of the poor of our continent.

SPEAKING OF GOD IN LATIN AMERICA

How are we to talk about a God who is revealed as love in a situation characterized by poverty and oppression? How are we to proclaim the God of life to men and women who die prematurely and unjustly? How are we to acknowledge that God makes us a free gift of love and justice when we have before us the suffering of the innocent? What words are we to use in telling those who are not even regarded as persons that they are the daughters and sons of God? These are key questions being asked in the theology that has been forming in Latin America and in other places throughout the world where the situation is the same.[8]

Bishop Desmond Tutu of Africa has spoken eloquently on this point:

Liberation theology more than any other kind of theology issues out of the crucible of human suffering and anguish. It happens because people cry out, "Oh, God, how long?" "Oh, God, but why? . . ." All liberation theology stems from trying to make sense of human suffering when those who suffer are the victims of organized oppression and exploitation, when they are emasculated and treated as less than what they are: human persons created in the image of the Triune God, redeemed by the one Savior Jesus Christ and sanctified by the Holy Paraclete. This is the genesis of all liberation theology and so also of black theology, which is theology of liberation in Africa.[9]

Human suffering, involvement with it, and the questions it raises about God are in fact one point of departure and one central theme in the theology of liberation. But the first concern in this context is not with the "evil of guilt" but rather with the "evil of misfortune," the evil suffered by the innocent. I am here using a distinction made by Adolphe Gesché, who remarks:

> The West has not had a theology of the evil of misfortune, the evil suffered by the innocent. In my view, the basic importance of the theology of liberation, that which gives it a major importance that I hope it will not lose, is that it takes into account the widespread, objective evil that entails no fault in the sufferer.[10]

I myself believe that we must not forget the responsibility of those who may be the cause of the evil suffered by the innocent. But Gesché's point is well taken: the suffering of the innocent and the questions it leads them to ask are indeed key problems for theology—that is, for discourse about God. The theology of liberation tries to meet the challenge.

The problem was already felt by those who empathized with the suffering of the Amerindians of Peru toward the end of the sixteenth century. Guamán Poma de Ayala tells us that he was moved by their plight and set out to scour the ancient Incan empire "in search of the poor of Jesus Christ." His mission led him to "settle among them for thirty years . . . and I went everywhere to see and promote justice and help for the poor." Faced with the injustices and indigence that he saw and heard of—"the poor of Jesus Christ are flayed and exploited"—Guamán Poma exclaims: "My God, where are you? Will you not hear me and help your poor, because I myself am helpless?"[11]

"My God, where are you?" is a question that springs from the suffering of the innocent, but it also has its source in faith. "It is precisely because they believe that their perplexity has arisen. . . . If they believed that God was neither good, nor loving, nor powerful, then there would be no problem. There would just be the brute fact of their suffering forming part of the givenness of a truly harsh reality."[12] The silence of God is hardest to bear for those who believe that the God of our faith is a living God and not like the "gods" of whom the psalmist says: "They have mouths, but do not speak" (Ps. 115:5).

Several centuries after Guamán Poma another witness, another "who swears to what his eyes have seen,"[13] tells us of the deep and boundless suffering of the Amerindians. José María Arguedas puts these words in the mouth of Ernesto, the character who represents him in his novel *Deep Rivers*:

Afterwards, when my father rescued me and I wandered with him through the towns, I found that people everywhere suffered. Perhaps the María Angola [the cathedral bell] mourned for all of them, here in Cuzco. I had never seen anyone more humiliated than the Old Man's *pongo* [unpaid Amerindian servant]. At every stroke the bell became more mournful and its sound penetrated everything.[14]

María Angola, made of gold and Amerindian blood, mourns and causes others to mourn. Its sad sound floods and penetrates everything. In that same cathedral is the Lord of the Earthquakes; his face resembles the faces of the most despised among the Amerindians, and in it is concentrated a vast sorrow:

The face of the crucified Christ was dark and gaunt, like that of the *pongo*. . . . Blackened, suffering, the Christ maintained a silence that did not set one at ease. He made one suffer; in such a vast cathedral, in the midst of the candle flames and the daylight that filtered down dimly, the countenance of the Christ caused suffering, extending it to the walls, to the arches and columns, from which I expected to see tears flow.[15]

In these descriptions the beauty of the language only underscores a profoundly cruel reality of long standing. The resemblance of the crucified Jesus and the Amerindian servant reminds us that the poor of Latin America (and elsewhere in the world) are "a crucified people."[16] We cannot be excused from taking this situation into account as we live and think our faith. This was the sure evangelical intuition of Bartolomé de Las Casas when he said that in the West Indies, they had abandoned "Jesus Christ, our God, scourging and grieving and striking and crucifying him, not once but thousands of times."[17]

But it is not only sadness that the bells of Cuzco's cathedral arouse. Ernesto says: "The bells brought cheer to the city. . . . Their happiness reigns throughout the church for the rest of the day." As it happens, the bells are located in the square known as "Pachacutek," the Incan word for "Renewer of the Earth." Therefore the square "glows with the radiance of heaven. Look how the light is reflected on us from the sides of the towers!" In this plaza "it may be that God is more at home . . . because the Incans chose it to be the center of the world." When the bells pealed, Ernesto went on to say, "the vibrations expanded . . . growing stronger, piercing the elements, transmuting everything into that Cuzco music that opened the doors to memory."

The great question is therefore this: How is it possible to arouse María Angola to enthusiasm and bring to the suffering the memory and joy of the risen Christ? That is, to proclaim, from this "center of the world," that sin and death have been overcome, so that we may speak of God and cause joy to reign in our time? Or, to make the point once again in the words of Arguedas: "So that the voice of the bells can rise up to heaven and return to earth with the song of the angel" that promises peace to all human beings of good will. And by "peace" I mean here all that is contained in the rich and complex Hebrew word *shālōm*: peace, security, justice, joy, life.

But if we are to proclaim the Easter joy bestowed by the victory of life over death, we must experience what Ernesto experienced and share the suffering of the least among human beings. Ernesto tells us:

> The ponderous tolling revived in my mind the humiliated image of the *pongo*, his deep-set eyes, the bones of his nose—the only energetic-looking thing about him—and his bare head with hair that seemed to be purposely tousled and covered with filth. "He has no father nor mother, only his shadow," I kept repeating to myself, remembering the words of a *huayno* [a folk song and dance of Incan origin], as with each step I awaited a new stroke of the immense bell.

The center of the world—so called because the crucified Jesus dwells there, and with him all who suffer unjustly, all the poor and despised of the earth—is the place from which we must proclaim the risen Lord.

THE BOOK OF JOB AND OURSELVES

I should like to go more deeply into this view of things with the aid of one of the most passionate and beautiful books of the Bible: the Book of Job. Ever since the time of the church fathers, the book's central character, the Job who suffers but continues to believe, has been regarded as one of the great prefigurations of Christ in the Hebrew scriptures. We have much to learn from him about our relationship of faith and hope with God and about the doing of theology.

Such a statement may surprise some readers. For there are those who regard other texts as far more relevant in relation to the poor of Latin America and commitment to their liberation from age-old oppression. Of what value is it in this context to reflect on a book that deals not with a historical act of deliverance but with theological considerations based on a literary fiction? On a book that is part of the sapiential literature of the Bible and seemingly so far removed from the problems of social justice? In point of fact, however, if this surprise exists it shows an ignorance of the biblical orientation that has characterized the theology of liberation from the outset. Above all, it signals a failure to grasp the connection between Christian life and the word of God.

Not only is it legitimate in principle to read the Bible from the standpoint of our deepest and most pressing concerns; this has also in fact been the practice of the Christian community throughout its history. But this principle and this fact must not make us forget something I have often said because I am deeply convinced of it: although it is true that we read the Bible, it is also true that the Bible reads us and speaks to us.[18] As the Letter to the Hebrews says, the scriptures x-ray us, so to speak: "The word of God is living and active, sharper than any two-edged sword, piercing to the division of soul and spirit, of joints and marrow, and discerning the thoughts and intentions of the heart" (4:12). Readiness to hear God as God speaks to us in this way is a necessary prerequisite if we are to be open not only to certain texts but to the Bible as a whole. If we lack this readiness we will in addition deprive ourselves of the riches contained in such books as Job, which deal with key points in the revelation of the God in whom we believe. The reading of scripture as members of the church always yields something new and unexpected.

In the following pages I shall be offering the reader an essay in theological reflection on Job. I am aware of the complexity and difficulty of this particular book;[19] it reveals its full grandeur and inner coherence only after a number of readings.[20] But I consider it worthwhile to accept the challenge the book represents, in order that I may call attention to certain points that I think can be very fruitful for the understanding of faith that is now being sought in Latin America. In so doing I shall adopt a standpoint that is dear to me, that of the connection, and even the identity, between theological methodology and spirituality.[21]

The themes that run through the Book of Job form a complex whole: the transcendence of God, the problem of evil, human suffering, the question of retribution, friendship, and others. The text contains all these themes and in consequence has inspired studies that put special emphasis on one or another aspect. The point of view that I myself adopt in this book is important and classic, and, I believe, central to the book itself: the question of *how we are to talk about God*. More particularly: how we are to talk about God from within a specific situation—namely, the suffering of the innocent. This focus is a very fruitful one and will enable us to penetrate to the heart of the Book of Job; in addition, it is consonant with my own concerns. In my discussion of the book I shall leave aside aspects and nuances that may be important in themselves in order to go directly to what interests me in this context. The Book of Job offers penetrating theological insights in the enchanting garb of poetry.[22]

In this reading of the Book of Job I shall keep my attention on what it means to talk of God in the context of Latin America, and more concretely in the context of the suffering of the poor—which is to say, the vast majority of the population.[23] The poor live their faith and proclaim their hope in the midst of what the Medellín and Puebla episcopal conferences call "inhuman misery" and "antievangelical poverty," resulting above all from unjust social structures that favor a privileged minority. The innocence that Job vigorously claims for himself helps us to understand the innocence of an oppressed and believing people amid the situation of suffering and death that has been forced upon it. But I shall also try to keep in mind other situations of personal suffering and grief.

In some lucid pages on Christ as "true witness," Karl Barth speaks of Job as having anticipated Christ in this witness. Barth also writes: "If . . . I recall certain passages [of the Book of Job] at the appropriate points in the section, it is less by way of illustration and more by way of indicating the actual sources of my whole line of thought."[24]

I can say something similar about the part played by the Latin American experience in my reading of Job. Explicit references to it will not be many; nonetheless this experience—and its present-day variations—are in a sense the source that points to a set of problems, raises questions, and guides the discussion, but this also, and above all, looks to the word of God for illumination and a response. My aim is not to make facile direct applications to the reality we face in Latin America but, with full respect for the text, to derive from the situation a perspective that will enable me to enter fully into the special message of this biblical book. The experience will be the backdrop for the pages that follow.

ON JOB

PART 1

The Wager

The Book of Job opens (1:1–2:13) and closes (42:7–17) with passages in prose that, like the side panels of an altarpiece, frame the more extensive central section, which is in verse (3:1–42:6).[1] Without these prose sections it is not possible to grasp the meaning of the polemical dialogues in this biblical book. In the narrative part the author gives us, in a few brief strokes, the key to the interpretation of his work. From a literary standpoint the book is built on a wager made with regard to talk about God.

Can human beings have a disinterested faith in God—that is, can they believe in God without looking for rewards and fearing punishments? Even more specifically: Are human beings capable, in the midst of unjust suffering, of continuing to assert their faith in God and speak of God without expecting a return? Satan, and with him all those who have a barter conception of religion, deny the possibility. The author, on the contrary, believes it to be possible, although he undoubtedly knew the difficulty that human suffering, one's own and that of others, raises against authentic faith in God. Job, whom he makes the vehicle of his own experiences, will be his spokesman.

In the end, God wins the wager. The rebellious but upright Job, in all his suffering and complaints, in his dogged commitment to the poor and his acknowledgment of the Lord's love, shows that his religion is indeed disinterested. But what path did he travel in finding the right way to speak of God? Can the route he followed be ours as well?

The poet wants to turn Job into an archetype, to make him the spokesman not of his personal experience alone but of the experience of all humankind. Living as I and many of my readers do in a continent where the suffering of the innocent is a massive reality, the wager on which the book is based has special meaning for us, and, without forgetting the book's universal significance, I shall be keeping this point in mind. Let us look first at the terms in which the wager is made in the Book of Job.

1

CHAPTER 1

"He Will Curse You to Your Face"

T he prologue tells us the story of "a sound and honest man [or: man of integrity and honesty] who feared God and shunned evil" (1:1).[1] At the same time, he possessed great material wealth. He was not a member of the Jewish people but a native of "the land of Uz" (1:1), which may have been part of Edom. This geographical location is further suggested by the names given to the friends of Job, for they refer to places in the same region.[2] The author wants to give his story a universal appeal that transcends national boundaries. As a matter of fact, the book does not explicitly mention either the chosen people or the covenant. The atmosphere is that of the patriarchal age, before the rise of Israel as a nation.[3]

At the outset the author notes the importance Job attributed to talk about God.[4] In his concern for his sons who were accustomed to giving frequent banquets, he would rise at dawn after such a banquet and "make a burnt offering for each of them. 'Perhaps,' Job would say, 'my sons have sinned and in their hearts blasphemed' " (1:5). The question of "speaking ill" and "speaking well" of God is thus a central one in the book.

THE INTEGRITY OF JOB

The first scene unfolded on earth, the second now takes place in the heavenly court, as the satan[5] makes his first wager. The angels, who are God's messengers, appear before him; among them, oddly enough, is the satan who has just been "prowling about on earth" (1:7). Yahweh proudly tells the satan how satisfied he is with the fidelity of Job: "Did you pay any attention to my servant Job? There is no one like him on the earth." He then repeats what we have already been told of Job: that he is a man of integrity and honesty, a man who fears God and shuns evil (1:8).

The terms are the same as in v. 1. The word I translate as "man of integrity" is the Hebrew *tām*, a term with a rich and complex meaning on which it will be

3

worth dwelling briefly. *Tām* means "innocent," but with the connotation of personal integrity, of something finished, complete, perfect, and therefore exemplary. Whence it also conveys the meaning "just."[6] Job's integrity will be acknowledged on several occasions (see, e.g., 2:3 and 2:9), and he himself will use the word *tām* (or its plural, *tāmim*) in proclaiming his innocence (see 9:20–21; 12:4; 27:5; 31:6). In addition to being called a "man of integrity"—a description that emphasizes the internal coherence of his personality—Job is also said to be "honest" (*yāshār*). This new adjective indicates his acceptance of ethical norms. Job is one who practices justice in his social life.[7]

If we add to this twofold characterization the second part of the sentence, "who fears God and shuns evil," we have a description of Job's *innocence* in relation to God and to his fellow human beings. The narrator states this innocence in v. 1, and God asserts it authoritatively in v. 8. The poet thus calls our attention to the integrity of Job from the opening lines of his book.

The satan then issues his challenges: "Yes, but Job is not God-fearing for nothing, is he? Have you not put a wall around him and his house and all his domain? You have blessed all he undertakes, and his flocks throng the country-side. But stretch out your hand and lay a finger on his possessions: then, I warrant you, he will curse you to your face" (1:9–11).

The challenge contains a point that is a key to the Book of Job. The text has to be read and analyzed carefully; otherwise the deeper meaning of the book will elude us.

It is impossible for the satan to deny that Job is a good and devout man. What he questions is rather the disinterestedness of Job's service of God, his lack of concern for a reward.[8] The satan objects not to Job's works but to their motivation: Job's behavior, he says, is not "for nothing" (in Hebrew: *hin-nām*).[9] In the satan's view, a religious attitude can be explained only by expectation of a reward; we will shortly learn that this is also the view of Job's friends. If, however, Job be regarded as a truly just man, then, even though there be no other like him in the land, the lie is given to this view of religion. The innocence of Job makes it historically possible that there may be other innocent human beings. The injustice of his suffering points to the possibility that other human beings may also suffer unjustly, and his disinterested outlook points to the possibility that others too may practice a disinterested religion.

Here we have the potential universality of the figure of Job; it is in fact clear that the poet intends to make a paradigm of him.[10] The satan, the obstacle, wishes to bar the way to this possibility, which implies the loving and completely free meeting of two freedoms, the divine and the human. It is this that gives the connection ("re-ligion") between the human person and God its full meaning as a disinterested self-surrender instead of a manipulation of the Lord to the human being's advantage.

With this in mind, the satan proposes his wager: "Lay a finger on his possessions: then, I warrant you, he will curse you to your face." Thus the central question of the Book of Job is raised at the outset: the role that reward or disinterestedness plays in faith in God and in its consistent implementation.

God believes that Job's uprightness is disinterested, and he therefore accepts the challenge. The author is telling us in this way that a utilitarian religion lacks depth and authenticity; in addition, it has something satanic about it (this is the first appearance of the irony that the author handles so skillfully). The expectation of rewards that is at the heart of the doctrine of retribution vitiates the entire relationship and plays the demonic role of obstacle on the way to God. In self-seeking religion there is no true encounter with God but rather the construction of an idol. When the friends of Job speak later on of rewards for those who reverence God (e.g., 8:5–7; 11:13–19), we will already know what to think. To believe "for nothing," "without payment," is the contrary of a faith based on the doctrine of retribution. This point will be bitterly debated in the subsequent dialogues.

The relationship between retribution and disinterestedness is therefore a theme that connects the prose section with the poetic section more closely than many interpreters think. This point will emerge with full clarity when I analyze the final discourses of God.[11] To put the matter quite concretely, the wager has to do with speaking of God in the light of the unjust suffering that seems, in human experience, to deny love on God's part. The terms and outcome of the challenge are given in the two narrative parts, thus enabling us to understand what the issue is in the language used of God in the poetic section.

As I said above, God accepts the satan's challenge because God trusts in Job. God says to the satan: "All he has is in your power. But keep your hands off his person" (1:12). At this point in the story, the scene changes again and we find ourselves once more on earth. Job receives news of the deaths of his sons and daughters and the loss of his possessions (1:13–19). Nonetheless, says the narrator, Job "committed no sin" and he "did not reproach God" (1:22). Yahweh is winning the bet.

After the enemy's first failure, God openly proclaims the innocence of Job amid his sufferings. He says to the satan: "He persists in his integrity still; you achieved nothing by provoking me to ruin him" (2:3). The innocence on which Job himself will insist so strongly later on is acknowledged by the Lord himself from the beginning of the book; we readers are fully informed of it. Furthermore, despite having been stricken in his possessions and his loved ones, Job "persists in his integrity still"; therefore his faith and behavior are disinterested, "for nothing." This is the point the author wishes to emphasize, because in his view disinterested religion alone is true religion.

DISINTERESTED RELIGION?

But the satan does not back down; he returns to the attack and challenges God once more. The earlier test was insufficient because, says the enemy, "Skin after skin! Someone will give away all he has to save his life. But stretch out your hand and lay a finger on his bone and flesh; I warrant you, he will curse you to your face" (2:5). Injury that touched only his possessions and family was not enough to make Job speak ill of God; now there is question of wounding him in his own body. The enemy continues to think that Job's piety and justice are not disinterested; that the reason he behaves as he does is the material rewards he has received; that his actions are not truly free and disinterested. The satan therefore feels more confident that this time, when he is able to attack the very person of Job, he will win the match. This is the last of the scenes in the heavenly court; henceforth everything (including the final revelation of God) will take place on earth.

Job falls ill. Afflicted "with malignant ulcers from the sole of his foot to the top of his head," he sits "among the ashes" (2:7–8). He is henceforth a sick as well as a poor man. To the death that is at work in his flesh there is added social death, for in the opinion of that time persons suffering from uncurable illnesses were to some extent outcasts from society.[12] A factor contributing to this attitude was the conviction that poverty and sickness were a punishment for the sins of the individual or the family.[13] In the eyes of his contemporaries, therefore, Job is a sinner and, because he had been a rich and important person, a great sinner. As a result, he is isolated and profoundly alone. He gives dramatic expression to his situation by making a place for himself outside the town on a garbage heap or dunghill. There, shortly afterward, he will voice his complaint and his lament.[14]

In view of this new calamity that has befallen Job, his wife—who is also affected by his misfortune and shares his unjust suffering—urges him to curse God. "Why persist in this integrity of yours? Curse God and die" (2:9).[15] The issue here is literally the *integrity* to which I have referred. What his wife challenges is Job's stubborn maintenance of his interior consistency and exemplary conduct.

Adversity does not cause him to lose his *innocence*. The author wants to make it clear that Job's perseverance in his religious outlook is a further expression of his disinterestedness, and so he pictures Job responding to his wife: "That is how a fool of a woman (*nābal*) talks" (2:10). The Bible describes as foolish or stupid those who deny God; that is why the psalmist says: "The fool thinks, 'There is no God' " (14:1). The denial of God that is meant here is not theoretical but practical; it is a rejection of God's just governance of the world and of the demands God makes on believers.[16]

Job refuses to utter such a denial, as the author expressly indicates: "In all this misfortune Job uttered no sinful word" (2:10). He did not speak ill, he did not curse. Job or, more correctly, God has won the wager: Job's religion is disinterested, he practices it "gratis."[17] But this does not end the matter. His response is sincere, but it will have to reach a deeper level. Our understanding of the attitude of disinterested faith, which gives the call to establish justice in history its true meaning, will be enriched by the experience of Job as he suffers and, at times, turns accuser.

This deeper response on Job's part, this deeper understanding of his faith, will require a passage through the dramatic crisis of which we are told in the poetic section of the book.

CHAPTER 2

Between Death and Life

T he final verses of the first prose section tell us that "the news of all the disasters that had fallen on Job reached the ears of three of his friends. Each of them set out from home—Eliphaz of Teman, Bildad of Shuah, and Zophar of Naamath—and by common consent they decided to go and offer him sympathy and consolation" (2:11). The intention of the newcomers is to share their friend's suffering and ease it to some degree. They will not desert him in his suffering, and to this extent they act meritoriously. They are serious, learned men, though perhaps oversure of their wisdom. They will try to explain to Job the reason for what is happening to him, because when adversity is understood it is easier to bear.

First, however, Job breaks a long silence with a monologue expressing his intense grief at a fate to which he would prefer death or not having been born. Despite this reaction, and as happens with other great sufferers, Job retains his hope in the God who gave him the gift of life.

FROM THE "GARBAGE HEAP"

The three friends were so moved by Job's plight that before they spoke they wept; then "they sat there on the ground beside him for seven days and seven nights. To Job they never spoke a word, for they saw how much he was suffering" (2:13). Their attitude was one of respectful compassion that showed how seriously they regarded their friend's situation. The silent sharing of suffering is a manifestation of fellowship.

At this point the poetic section of the book begins. It comprises lengthy speeches by Job, his friends, a new and unexpected personage named Elihu, and, finally, God. The purpose of the speeches is to discover the meaning of God's behavior in relation to what happens to the central figure of the book and in human life generally.

Job's misfortune continues and seems to intensify beyond what was indicated in his initial reaction to it. The monologue that opens the most substantial part of the book is characterized by great poetic beauty and gives heartrending expression to this gradual immersion in suffering.[1] The opening

7

lines already set the tone: "In the end it was Job who broke the silence and cursed the day of his birth. This is what he said: 'Perish the day on which I was born and the night that told of a boy conceived' " (3:1–3).

There is question here once more of speaking: Job curses the day of his birth. He does not curse God, but he does complain about God. He experiences his suffering as an abandonment by God.[2] He therefore wishes that night might swallow him up; that the world might be covered with darkness; that all might revert to its precreation state when "the earth was without form and void, and darkness was on the face of the deep" (Gen. 1:2) and God had not yet said: "Let there be light" (Gen. 1:3):[3]

> May that day be darkness,
>   may God on high have no thought for it,
>   may no light shine on it.
> May murk and shadow dark as death claim it for their
>   own,
>   clouds hang over it,
>   eclipse swoop down on it.
> See! Let obscurity seize on it,
>   from the days of the year let it be excluded,
>   into the reckoning of the months not find its way
>   [3:4–6].

Job's suffering causes him to see the universe as chaotic, as lacking the presence of God; from it God is absent as the one who creates it and shapes it into a cosmos. But Job goes further: he looks for an impossible retrogression to the time before his birth. He asks why they let him be born:

> Why was I not still-born,
>   or why did I not perish as I left the womb? . . .
> Why give light to a man of grief?
>   Why give life to those bitter of heart,
> who long for a death that never comes,
>   and hunt for it more than for buried treasure?
> They would be glad to see the grave-mound
>   and shout for joy if they reached the tomb.
> Why give light to one who does not see his way,
>   whom God shuts in all alone? [3:11, 20–23].

Faced with the reality of his present existence, Job would prefer death or, even better, never to have been born.[4] Moreover, in his experience human life seems so chaotic that there can be no solution to social inequalities—except in the realm of death. The call for justice that plays an important part in the Book of Job, as we shall see, is here presented in an ironic connection with death:

Down there, the wicked bustle no more,
  there the weary rest.
Prisoners, all left in peace,
  hear no more the shouts of the oppressor.
High and low are there together,
  and the slave is free of his master [3:17–19].

The meaning is not that Job chooses death against life as seen in the dichotomy presented in Deuteronomy: "This day . . . I have set before you life and death, blessing and curse; therefore choose life, that you and your descendants may live, loving the Lord your God, obeying his voice, and cleaving to him; for that means life to you" (Deut. 30:19–20). Rather, Job finds that "for me, there is no calm, no peace; my torments banish rest" (3:26), and to this he would prefer not to have been born. In a sense, he is trying to locate himself in a time before the choice between life and death, in the time before birth. That is how far his suffering drives him.

"I AM GOING TO TALK ABOUT HOPE"

Job's response is so radical as to be baffling; it can have sprung only from a very deep and unbearable misery. Existence, after all, is a gift of the God of life. What, then, can it mean to desire not to have received this divine gift?[5] The author may have been inspired by the prophet Jeremiah[6] who in a famous passage uses expressions very like those of Job:

Cursed be the day
  on which I was born!
The day when my mother bore me,
  let it not be blessed!
Cursed be the man
  who brought the news to my father,
"A son is born to you,"
  making him very glad.
Let that man be like the cities
  which the Lord overthrew without pity;
let him hear a cry in the morning
  and an alarm at noon,
because he did not kill me in the womb;
  so my mother would have been my grave,
  and her womb for ever great.
Why did I come forth from the womb
  to see toil and sorrow,
  and spend my days in shame? [Jer. 20:14–18].

The cries of Jeremiah and Job are cries of torment in a cruel situation. "What wonder then," Job will say, "if my words are wild?" (6:3); they are not a rejection of God. In fact, it might well be claimed that this manifestation of irrepressible feeling expresses, even if in an unconventional form, a profound act of self-surrender and hope in God.[7] It springs from a situation of suffering that has no intelligible cause. César Vallejo puts it in blank verse in his *Trilce*: "My pain is so deep that it never had a cause, and has no need of a cause. What could its cause have been? Where is that thing so important that it stopped being its cause? Its cause is nothing, and nothing could have stopped being its cause. Why has this pain been born all on its own?"[8]

To a superficial reader, the paradoxical thing about this poem is the surprising title Vallejo gives it: "I am going to talk about hope." The hope is doubtless one that does not travel beaten paths, but it is not therefore any less firm; it is a hope that is unaccompanied by any boastful rational grasp of things and yet is clear-eyed. Vallejo's poem, like the poet's own life, expresses the deep, inexplicable suffering of the Latin American poor. In this case, the historical bewilderment and sadness of the indigenes as they saw the vital framework of their world collapsing[9] is accompanied today by the exploitation and despoliation of the ordinary people. But the poem also shows the stubborn hope that gives heart to this poor, believing people.

Job may have been led to his monologue in like manner. A profound experience underlies its heartfelt and candid expression of suffering. He will have occasion to reveal this experience during the grueling debate that begins after this passage.[10] Despite his sometimes cutting and bitter complaints and protests, he does not in fact despair, as we shall see.

CHAPTER 3

Job Spoke Well

J ob's debate with his friends will not be polished in its manner; we shall have an opportunity to see it unfold. In the second prose section, after the lengthy speeches are finished, God will say that Job, unlike his friends (Elihu is not mentioned), has "spoken correctly of me" (42:7 and 42:8). That was precisely the subject of the debate: How to speak of God. God will twice say as much, just as there had been two attempts to make Job curse God.[1] The satan has lost his wager concerning the possibility of disinterested religion, for Job continues to cling to the Lord in his suffering and even when he comes close to despair; he does not speak ill of God, he does not curse God. On the contrary, with an effort and through trial and error, he is able to find the appropriate words. The problem of speaking correctly about God amid unjust suffering is not limited to the case of Job, but is a challenge to every believer. This is especially true of situations in which the suffering reaches massive proportions. In Latin America the suffering has given rise to a special theological approach.

THE SUFFERING OF THE INNOCENT

God's approval evidently refers to Job's speeches as a whole, to the entire way he has followed. As we shall see, these speeches do not lack for bold expressions that spring from the depths of Job's suffering and from the torment he feels at not being able to understand what has happened to him. But these bold expressions do not prevent God's agreement and approval; God does not accuse Job either of sin in his earlier life or of blasphemy in what he has said. This is a first surprise for Job's friends, who had been convinced they were defending God against Job. God has won—this time for good—the wager that the satan had made with God (it is significant that the satan does not reappear in the final prose section).

Furthermore, if the friends, attached as they are to their own teaching and certainties, thought that they could interpret God's words as favoring their point of view, God now eliminates this possibility once and for all. God says to

Eliphaz of Teman: "I burn with anger against you and against your two friends." They have not known how to speak correctly of God, and God therefore orders them to offer animals as a burnt offering for their fault.

Furthermore, in a second and even greater surprise for these conceited theologians, God tells them that only the intercession of the upright Job can save them from punishment: they are to offer their sacrifices while Job prays for them. God will hear his prayers and not punish them as their folly (*nēbālah*) deserves (42:8).

The author here displays once again the biting humor that enables him to underscore the message he wants to get across: those who claimed to be God's defenders are now the accused (on one occasion Job tells his friends that they are defending God "by prevarication and by dishonest argument"—13:7). In addition, they now need the intercession of the irreverent Job if God is not to hold them to account for their "folly" (*nēbālah*, with overtones of "blasphemy").[2] It is to be noted that the same word was used (in adjectival form) to describe the attitude of Job's wife in the prologue (see 2:10).[3] We are thus in the presence of a new and stinging irony: the friends with their carefully developed theological speeches have not in fact produced more than spontaneously foolish and indeed almost blasphemous responses to the situation.[4]

Yahweh subsequently gives Job back his family, his possessions, and his health. The ending evidently displays a certain naivety,[5] but it should be emphasized that the poet wants to give human and material expression to the deep spiritual joy that Job has experienced in his final encounter with God (in 42:2–6). Karl Barth therefore calls Yahweh's action a "concrete confirmation" of the innocence and uprightness of Job.[6]

How are human beings to speak of God in the midst of poverty and suffering? This is the question the Book of Job raises for us. An upright man living a prosperous, happy life is reduced to wretchedness and sickness. The key question is therefore: How will Job speak of God in this situation? Will he reject God? Have Job's piety and uprightness perhaps been really based on his material prosperity? Will he curse God for having destroyed all that prosperity?

There is evidently more at issue here than the plight of one individual. The question just asked in regard to Job can be put in a broader and more radical form: How are human beings to find a language applicable to God in the midst of innocent suffering? This question, with all its implications for our understanding of the justice and unmerited generosity of God, is the great theme of the Book of Job. Throughout the work Job will stubbornly insist on his innocence. How, then, is a human being to speak of God and to God in the situation that Job must endure?

We ask the same question today in the lands of want and hope that are Latin America. Here the masses of the poor suffer an inhuman situation that is evidently undeserved. Nothing can justify a situation in which human beings lack the basic necessities for a life of dignity and in which their most elementary rights are not respected. The suffering and the destructive effect on individuals go far beyond what is seen in a first contact with the world of the poor. In such a situation, what content can be assigned to the "Abba, Father!" (literally: "Abba, Papa!") that the Spirit cries within us (see Gal. 4:6)? How are we to proclaim the reign of love and justice to those who live in an inexplicable situation that denies this reign? How are we to bring joyous conviction to our utterance of the name of God?

It is important that we be clear from the outset that the theme of the Book of Job is not precisely suffering—that impenetrable human mystery—but rather how to speak of God in the midst of suffering. The question that concerns the author is the possibility of disinterested religion, of believing "for nothing"; in his view only a faith and behavior of this kind can be offered to a God who loves freely and gratuitously. But is it possible?

In dealing with the subject, the poet does not make things easy for himself. In order to contemplate the possibility, he chooses the most difficult of all human situations, that of physical and moral suffering. On the one hand, in such a situation there is a great temptation to seek personal interests and to judge the situation in terms of rewards and punishments. We know from experience that our misfortunes make us turn in upon ourselves and see ourselves as the center to which all must be related: other persons and even God, whom we thus idolatrously turn into our servant. On the other hand, if the element of injustice be added to this situation of suffering, it can produce resentment and a rejection of the presence and existence of God, because God's love becomes difficult to understand for one living a life of unmerited affliction. The result, then, in both cases is a radical questioning of God.

In recent times, few have voiced the second of these difficulties as austerely and persistently as Albert Camus. According to Camus, there is no place for God in a world so pervaded by the suffering of the innocent. In *The Plague*, in which the presence of evil in the world is the key to interpreting everything, Camus reports one of his characters saying, in a sermon:

> Truth to tell, nothing was more important on earth than a child's suffering, the horror it inspires in us, and the reasons we must find to account for it. In other manifestations of life God made things easy for us and, thus far, our religion had no merit. But in this respect He put us, so to speak, with our backs to the wall. Indeed, we were all up against the wall that plague had built around us, and in its lethal shadow we must work out our salvation.

The decisive choice must be made when we are up against the wall of the plague and faced with the suffering of the innocent. As Fr. Paneloux, the Jesuit preacher, puts it: "My brothers, a time of testing has come for us all. We must believe everything or deny everything. And who among you, I ask, would dare to deny everything?"[7]

Camus makes a tremendous, heartbreaking effort to deny everything. In his play, *The Misunderstanding*, an unfortunate mistake leads to the murder of

Jan by his mother and his sister Martha. At the end, in contrast to the rebellious toughness of Martha, Jan's wife Maria (the names are revealingly symbolic) utters a prayer, the only one to be found in the works of Camus: "Oh, God, I cannot live in this desert! It is on You that I must call, and I shall find the words to say. [*She sinks on her knees.*] I place myself in your hands. Have pity on me, and turn toward me. Hear me and raise me from the dust. O heavenly Father! Have pity on those who love each other and are parted." The answer to this plea is coldly definitive; it is the answer of the deaf servant ("the old manservant"): "No." This no is the final word of the play; it symbolizes God's deafness, God's silence in the face of human suffering. More accurately, it is a no to the existence of a God who can permit this suffering.[8]

Camus returns over and over to the theme of innocent suffering. He encounters dilemmas and self-criticisms in his search,[9] but the problem remains, a source of suffering and a challenge to everyone.

There is in fact no circumstance of human life that makes it more difficult to accept the gratuitous love of God than our own experience of suffering, especially if the suffering be unjust. For this reason (the author of the Book of Job seems to say), if believers caught in this situation are able to live their faith disinterestedly and find language suitable for speaking of God, then human beings can accept the God of the Bible without being unfaithful to themselves. This is the wager on which the Book of Job is built and to which the poet tries to respond. He takes the bull by the horns. Any attempt that does not start with this ultimate situation will fail to induce conviction, for the nagging suspicion that motivates the satan's wager will not be silenced: "Do you think his religion is disinterested? Touch him, and he will curse you."[10]

The Book of Job is a literary construct, but it could have been written only by someone who had suffered in flesh and spirit. Job's protesting lament bears the seal of personal experience; so do his confrontation with God and his final surrender and new certainty. The work is written with a faith that has been drenched in tears and reddened by blood. This champion of the gratuitousness of God's love is like Paul of Tarsus in that he has known suffering and loneliness. The Book of Job with its lights and shadows, its success and its limitations, reflects a personal odyssey.

Job is not a patient man, at least not in the usual sense of the word. He is rather a rebellious believer. His rebellion is against the suffering of the innocent, against a theology that justifies it, and even against the depiction of God that such a theology conveys. But if human beings cannot be condemned in order to defend God, neither can God be condemned in order to defend human beings.[11] Job learns this gradually. In the process he will become a believer who possesses the peace to which the contemplation of God ultimately leads him.[12] It is a peace that does not lessen the importance of his call for justice (on the contrary, he "spoke correctly") and is therefore authentic. In this sense, Job the rebel is a witness to peace and to the hunger and thirst for justice (those who live thus will one day be called "blessed"); he is more than simply patient, he is a peace-loving man, a peacemaker.

Precisely because the author has himself shared Job's experience, he does not seek an ultimate rational explanation of human suffering; neither, however, does he look upon suffering as simply a pretext for discussing other themes. Rather he accepts it with all its meaning, confusion, and implications for something that lies deep, very deep, in his soul: his faith and hope in Yahweh. He knows, as his vivid descriptions make clear, that the suffering of the innocent is the most inhuman of all possible situations. He therefore confronts it and asks whether in view of it he can still acknowledge the God whose gratuitous exercise of freedom brings fulfillment to our humanity.

TALKING OF GOD

This, then, is the question: Are suffering human beings able to enter into an authentic relationship with God and find a correct way of speaking about God? If the answer is yes, then it will be a priori possible to do the same in other human situations. But if the answer is no, then it will be irrelevant that persons living in less profound and challenging situations "appear" to accept the gratuitousness of God's love and claim to practice a disinterested religion. Human suffering is the harsh, demanding ground on which the wager about talk of God is made; it is also that which ensures that the wager has universal applicability.

A comparison with another famous wager, that of Blaise Pascal, may shed some light here. In Pascal's case, the wager has to do with the existence or nonexistence of God. The question Pascal asks is: "Which will you choose?"[13] In Job the choice is between a religion based on the rights and obligations of human beings as moral agents, and a disinterested belief based on the gratuitousness of God's love. Pascal employs a crystal-clear, almost mathematical logic in responding to the questionings of the modern mind and the first manifestations of unbelief. In Job the challenges arising from the suffering of the innocent are met in a tortuous trial in which progress is made through a series of violent jolts. Pascal warns that a choice must be made between unbelief and God, and points out that not to choose is to choose: "You must wager. There is no choice; you are already committed." In Job the choice is between a religion that sets conditions for the action of God and applies a calculus to it, and a faith that acknowledges the free initiative at work in God's love; to make no choice is to live in despair or cynicism.

As Pascal sees it, modern men and women have to understand that belief in God is to their advantage:

Since you must necessarily choose, your reason is no more affronted by choosing one rather than the other. . . . Let us weigh up the gain and the loss involved in calling heads that God exists. Let us assess the two cases: if you win you win everything, if you lose you lose nothing. Do not hesitate then; wager that he does exist.

In the Book of Job, to be a believer means sharing human suffering, especially that of the most destitute, enduring a spiritual struggle, and finally accepting the fact that God cannot be pigeonholed in human categories. In Pascal's wager, he addresses human beings who are proud of their reasoning powers, and he tries to make them see how limited these powers are and how great is their need of God: "Concentrate then," he urges his supposed interlocutor, "not on convincing yourself by multiplying proofs of God's existence but by diminishing your passions." In Job there is question of telling the innocent who are beset by unjust suffering that God loves them and that their legitimate demand for justice for themselves and others acquires its fullest measure and greatest urgency in the universe of gratuitousness.

Pascal issues his shrewd and subtle wager to unbelievers; the wager in Job thrusts with beautiful radicality into the world of nonpersons. Pascal incisively confronts the winners of history; with tender compassion, the Book of Job seeks out its losers. Pascal's wager is the first step in a fruitful theological line that even today meets the challenges of modernity;[14] the wager in Job starts on the "garbage heap" (see 2:10, *mazbaleh*) of the city to look for a suitable language for talking of God.[15] Situated as we are on the underside of history here in Latin America, it is the second wager that is ours: to speak of God from the standpoint of the poor of the earth.

The path followed in the Book of Job to what is divinely certified as correct language about God is illuminating and a stimulus to us.[16] As the path unfolds, various kinds of theological discourse are used in the attempt to explain what has befallen Job. They represent different ways of rendering an account of faith in God.

Two major shifts of viewpoint take place in Job's way of speaking as he tormentedly rejects the doctrine of retribution in the light of his personal experience. The first occurs when, at the instigation of his friends, he broadens his perspective, abandons his initial narrow position, and realizes that the issue here is not simply the suffering of one individual. The real issue, he sees, is the suffering and injustice that mark the lives of the poor. Those who believe in God must therefore try to lighten the burden of the poor by helping them and practicing solidarity with them. The speeches of God occasion the second shift: Job now understands that the world of justice must be located within the broad but demanding horizon of freedom that is formed by the gratuitousness of God's love.

Two types of language thus emerge as the two closest approximations to a correct language about God: the language of prophecy and the language of contemplation. In saying this, I am not attempting to "rationalize" unduly a work that is deeply poetic and rich in nuances. In the Book of Job the two languages mentioned both absorb and are opposed to other ways of speaking of God. They move apart and they intermingle; they move forward and at times they turn back. But despite this complexity, which is a sign of the book's great richness, a progress and maturation is observable in the book as a whole. It is not true, as is sometimes said, that the speeches circle repetitively around a few basic questions. On the contrary, there are important advances and changes of tone in the several rounds of speeches and as the various personages of the story make their appearance. The poet is trying by this means to find an answer to questions about faith and life.

I wish to emphasize this element of gradual maturation as the book moves along. At the same time, however, I am aware that from some points of view the initial question about speaking of God remains open; indeed, it is too profound a question for this not to be the case. "My thoughts are not your thoughts, neither are your ways my ways, says the Lord" (Isa. 55:8). We are repeatedly called upon to face the unexpected.

It must also be said that the question calls for answers at other levels, for in fact more than language is at issue. Talk about God presupposes and, at the same time, leads to a living encounter with God in specific historical circumstances. It requires, therefore, that we discover the features of Christ in the sometimes disfigured faces of the poor of this world. This discovery will not be made apart from concrete gestures of solidarity with our brothers and sisters who are wretched, abandoned, and deprived.

But the mystery of God is not exhausted by its historical embodiment. The Apostle Paul tells us: "Now we see in a mirror dimly, but then face to face. Now I know in part; then I shall understand fully, even as I have been fully understood" (1 Cor. 13:12). In this book I am looking in a mirror and accepting the limitations the mirror imposes. These pages are inspired by the hope that a time will come when shadows and reflections disappear and we shall see face to face, knowing as we are in turn known. Love, the virtue (that is, the power) that will win out in the end, stirs us even now to a spirit of joyous thanksgiving for the gift of God's love.

PART 2

The Language
of Prophecy

The author of the Book of Job bitterly disputes the traditional doctrine of temporal retribution. The debate on this point occupies a good part of the work or even, in a way, the whole of it; but the rejection of the doctrine is not a simple matter, for the classic position seems to be supported by a solid theology.

In the course of the discussion, Job, who in the final analysis is carrying on his dialogue more with God than with his friends, broadens the basis on which he judges and comes to see his case as related to that of other sufferers, especially the poor. As a result he realizes that relatedness to God implies a relatedness to the poor. He then reviews his past life in a new monologue: in that past life he practiced justice and could therefore enjoy an intimacy with the Lord. His present situation continues to be profoundly incomprehensible to him, but nonetheless a prophetic way of speaking about God begins to emerge.

A spirited personage comes on the scene. He talks of the pedagogical value of suffering, but he also repeats, and with some vigor, the attention the poor deserve from God.

CHAPTER 4

Sorry Comforters

T he companionable silence of the three friends is broken after Job's monologue. The three men are scandalized by what they have heard. Job (they think) is delirious; he has spoken out of the bitterness caused by his suffering and without repentance for his sin. Yet, that he is himself responsible for his plight is evident to these friendly theologians who now begin to argue along this line. The doctrinal context in which they think is that of temporal retribution. Job has the same theoretical point of reference, but his experience and his faith in God have finally shattered this theology for him. His consciousness of his own integrity is incompatible with it. He begins to glimpse a way, a method, for speaking of God.

"HEAR AND APPLY TO YOURSELF"

When all is said and done, if Job is not guilty, how is it possible to explain what has befallen him? His friends want to help him, but they cannot do so except on the basis of their own vision of things, their own theology. Eliphaz, leader of the group, speaks to counsel his unfortunate friend. He knows his words will seem harsh to Job, but he also knows that he must offer correct teaching:

> If we say something to you, will you bear with us?
> Who in any case could refrain from speaking now?
> [4:2].

The core of this teaching, which Eliphaz and his companions expound with unshakable conviction, is that God punishes the wicked and rewards the upright. The principle of cause and effect applies inexorably in the moral world. Eliphaz challenges Job:

21

> Can you recall anyone guiltless that perished?
> Where then have the honest been wiped out?
> I speak from experience: those who plough iniquity
> and sow disaster reap just that [4:7-8].

Riches and health on the one side, poverty and sickness on the other, are what God decrees, respectively, for those who live virtuously or unvirtuously. In the case of Job, the problem is to apply this principle, but working backward: if Job suffers as he does, then he is a sinner, though he may not be aware of it. The logic allows no exceptions. It is so clear that Eliphaz can even appeal to experience to illustrate the argument: "Can you recall?" and "I speak from experience" refer to concrete situations.[1]

The ethico-religious conception that Eliphaz invokes is based on the idea of temporal retribution.[2] One purpose of the author of the book is to challenge this conception by showing it to be inoperative and misleading. For the moment, Job is pressured by his friends to accept it and apply it to his own case. Eliphaz offers theological arguments in the name of all three friends and he concludes as one sure of his position: "All this we have searched out and it is so! Hear and apply to yourself" (5:27).[3] Before speaking he has made an effort to find out the truth of the matter; now he does not fail to draw the necessary inferences from it.[4] He is firm, but still friendly.

The point is clear: the impoverishment and sickness that Job is suffering are punishments for his sins. Mortals who deny this truth are claiming to be more righteous than God (4:17). Job's first duty, therefore, is to acknowledge his sin and ask God's forgiveness for it. Eliphaz suggests that he repent: "If I were you, I should appeal to God and lay my case before him" (5:8). It is a call to conversion that Job ignores because he finds no guilt in himself.

Bildad and Zophar then speak their piece in turn after Job's reply to the previous speaker; they repeat Eliphaz's arguments, adding little new. The three men are convinced of the doctrine of temporal retribution;[5] as the dispute continues, they grow angry at Job's resistance and their speeches become both repetitious and aggressive.

The ethical pattern they expound is a simple one that can be applied in a highly individualistic way. Its power flows precisely from its simplicity. It was the prevailing doctrine at the period when the author of the Book of Job was writing, and it has cropped up repeatedly wherever a particular religious mentality has been at work. It is, moreover, a convenient and soothing doctrine for those who have great worldly possessions, and it promotes resignation and a sense of guilt in those who lack such possessions. In the course of the history of the Church certain tendencies in the Christian world have repeatedly given new life to the ethical doctrine that regards wealth as God's reward to the honest and the hard-working, and poverty as God's punishment to the sinful and the lazy.[6]

On the other hand, as everyone knows, the capitalist ideology has historically made use of this doctrinal expedient—openly in the beginning; nowadays in more subtle forms—for its own religious justification.[7] This manipulation of the doctrine distorts one point in it that continues to be important despite all criticisms of the teaching—namely, that the Christian faith necessarily entails a personal and social ethic. I shall return to this point.

I AM INNOCENT

The friends' replies elicit a violent response from Job. They also help him, however, to broaden his own horizon, refine his arguments against the doctrine of retribution, and discover new perspectives.

The fact is that at the theoretical level Job himself accepts the prevailing ethical doctrine of his age as expressed in the speeches of his friends; he does not, however, feel as sure of it as they do. His doubts about it come from his own painful experience, but they do not lead him to deny God. He says sadly to Eliphaz:

> If only my misery could be weighed,
>   and all my ills be put together on the scales!
> But they outweigh the sands of the seas:
>   what wonder then if my words are wild? . . .
> Will no one hear my prayer,
>   will not God himself grant my hope?
> May it please God to crush me,
>   to give his hand free play and do away with me!
> This thought, at least, would give me comfort
>   (a thrill of joy in unrelenting pain),
>   that I never rebelled against the Holy One's decrees
>   [6:2–3, 8–10].

Job expresses his exultation with a certain pride: he has not blasphemed. Nonetheless he sees that his words of complaint may have gone beyond what he intended. But in the midst of his sufferings he has no other way of expressing himself, and therefore he pleads to be heard and given an answer. He feels more alone than ever. The discussion begun with his friends has quickly turned into a dialogue of the deaf. The doctrine these theologians profess does not allow them to hear what others are saying; the echo of their own words stops up their ears. Job says to them:

> Will no one teach you to be quiet
>   —the only wisdom that becomes you!
> Kindly listen to my accusation
>   and give your attention to the way I shall plead
>   [13:5–6].

If these men were to be silent and listen, they would demonstrate the wisdom they claim to possess. Those who experience at close range the sufferings of the poor, or of anyone who grieves and is abandoned, will know the importance of what Job is asking for. The poor and the marginalized have a deep-rooted conviction that no one is interested in their lives and misfortunes. They also have the experience of receiving deceptive expressions of concern from persons who in the end only make their problems all the worse.

This is why in the basic ecclesial communities of Latin America, for example, many find to their surprise that their difficulties, especially those of which they say little, matter to others. This creates for them an unwonted space or possibility of freedom and communication that prepares them for receiving the word of the Lord and also for becoming active in their own history. This is the space or possibility Job asks for himself.

Later on, Job will accept with humble resignation that others should laugh at him, but he pleads that at least they should first listen to him:

> Listen carefully to my words;
>   let this be the consolation you allow me.
> Permit me to speak in my turn;
>   you may jeer when I have spoken [21:2-3].[8]

In his resolute defense of his innocence, Job does not make the mistake of regarding himself as sinless. At different points he recognizes that as a fallible human being he is not without his shortcomings (see 7:21; 13:26). In God's sight we are all sinners:

> And this is the creature on whom you fix your gaze,
>   and bring to judgement before you!
> But will anyone produce the pure from what is impure?
> No one can! [14:3-4].

The point is rather that when Job examines himself he finds no sin that merits so great a punishment; in view therefore of his own experience, he disputes the theological explanation current in the period when the book was written. His friends' arguments, which are based on a particular view of justice, only intensify his consciousness of being innocent; as he listens to them, his conviction grows that he is an upright man. The question for Job is not whether or not he is a sinner; he knows well that as a human being he is indeed a sinner. The question rather is whether he deserves the torments he is suffering. His answer is unambiguous: no, he does not deserve them.

All this means that the point at issue has shifted. It is no longer simply the suffering of the poor and the sick, of which he spoke in his monologue. He has thought out the matter more fully; the issue is more specifically the misfortune of the innocent. We are confronted now with suffering that is unjust. As a result, the question "Why?" becomes even more heartrending and a source of even greater tension. The arguments of the friends sound hollow as they dash against Job's conviction of his innocence. The reason for Job's intensifying rebelliousness is not so much his own sufferings as the justifications his interlocutors give for them:

> Put me right, and I shall say no more;
>   show me where I have been at fault.
> Fair comment can be borne without resentment,
>   but what are your strictures aimed at?
> Do you think mere words deserve censure,
>   desperate speech that the wind blows away?
> Soon you will be haggling over the price of an orphan,
>   and selling your friend at bargain price!
> Come, I beg you, look at me:
>   man to man, I shall not lie.
> Relent then, no harm is done;
>   relent then, since I am upright [6:24–29].

The ironic, biting tone is in response to the friends who discourse so superficially and give precedence to words over human beings subjected to suffering. What respect does so abstract and cold a doctrine deserve? On the other hand, the conviction of innocence that Job so emphatically repeats does not fit in with the ethical doctrine of retribution.[9] For if his life has been an upright one, why have poverty and sickness befallen him? Is God unjust in punishing him? The question is an agonizing one. Job has no clear answer to it; at times he seems to imply that the Lord is indeed unjust, but he never says it in so many words. What is certain is that his consciousness of being innocent conflicts with the ethico-religious view he too has accepted until now. His friends reproach him for being inconsistent; they even try to make him see that he is blaspheming. They realize what his protestation of innocence implies in their view of things, and they are scandalized.

Eliphaz voices this accusation at the beginning of the second round of speeches (chapters 15–21), which display a greater aggressiveness of the friends toward Job. The contrast with the first set of speeches is great. The tone has changed. No longer do the three men offer advice and remind a friend in misfortune that he should acknowledge his sin. Job's stubbornness has angered them; his words of self-defense have undone him in their eyes. He is now a defendant. The inference Eliphaz draws from Job's imprudent self-justification is in his view irresistible: in proclaiming himself to be innocent, Job is opposing God:

> Eliphaz of Teman spoke next. He said:
> "Does anyone wise respond with windy arguments,
>   or feed on an east wind?
> Or make a defence with ineffectual words
>   and speeches good for nothing?

> You do worse: you suppress reverence,
>   you discredit discussion before God.
> Your very fault incites you to speak like this,
>   hence you adopt this language of cunning.
> Your own mouth condemns you, and not I;
>   your own lips bear witness against you. . . .
> You vent your anger on God
>   and speeches come tripping off your tongue!
> How can anyone be pure,
>   anyone born of woman be upright? [15:1–6, 13–14].

In this view Job has slandered God; the satan has therefore won his wager. Job does not speak truthfully and respectfully of the traditional doctrine. It is not possible to speak correctly of God in the language of the cunning. "Cunning" (artfulness, craftiness) has a negative connotation here (this is not always the case in the Bible). Eliphaz had used the word with the same meaning in his first speech when he said that God "frustrates the plans of the artful, so that they cannot succeed in their intrigues" (5:12).[10] Job is thus doing away with fear of God, which is the very root of the religious outlook. There can be no greater boldness, no greater perversion of faith in God. His own words condemn him.

Job is not intimidated, however, for he knows that this is not at all certain. All he wants is to ask questions inspired by his suffering. Shortly before the speech of Eliphaz that was cited a moment ago, at the point when Job was starting hostilities with the three friends, he had said sarcastically:

> Doubtless, you are the voice of the people,
>   and when you die, wisdom will die with you!
> But I have a brain as well as you.
>   I am in no way inferior to you,
>   and who, in any case, does not know all that?
>   [12:2–3].

There is no question then of denying God but only of challenging an interpretation of the relationship between human beings and God that bases it on retribution. Job is familiar with the doctrine and had perhaps accepted it in the past. It does not, however, explain his present experience, nor is it in accord with the deepest insights of his faith:

> I have seen all this with my own eyes,
>   heard with my own ear and understood.
> Whatever you know, I know too;
>   I am in no way inferior to you.
> But my words are intended for Shaddai;
>   I mean to remonstrate with God.
> As for you, you are only charlatans,
>   all worthless as doctors [13:1–4].

As the discussion proceeds, Job becomes aware that the dividing line between himself and his interlocutors lies in the area of personal experience and
of the thinking that experience yields. He does not see his way clear, but he does
have the honesty and courage to seek further. His friends prefer to repeat ideas
they learned in the past, instead of turning to the concrete lives of living
persons, asking questions, and in this way opening themselves to a better
understanding of God and God's word. The result is that their arguments are
simply a medley of lies arranged to seem like the truth. Job is not afraid to say
as much; his friends' speeches are a further reason to break off the debate with
them and address himself directly to God.

TWO THEOLOGICAL METHODS

As we read the speeches of Job and his friends, it becomes clear that we are in
the presence of two types of theological reasoning. The author is not satisfied
that his readers would see this; he will have his principal character likewise
become clearly and explicitly aware of the issue.

The speeches of Eliphaz and his companions take certain doctrinal principles as their starting point and try to apply them to Job's case. At the end of his
opening speech Eliphaz says this to Job with an assurance he intends should be
contagious:

> All this we have observed and it is so!
> Heed it, you will be the wiser for it! [5:27].

These men are competent, even if mistaken, theologians; they are convinced
of their teaching but they are unaware that it has nothing to say to suffering
human beings. In their view Job's duty is to understand this theology, accept it,
and apply it to his own situation; only in this way will he reach interior peace. If
he continues to complain, he will only worsen his situation. In the second series
of speeches, which, as I said before, show an increasing hostility between the
interlocutors, Bildad speaks angrily, but with a certain smugness:

> What prevents you others from saying something?
> Think—for it is our turn to speak!
> Why do you regard us as animals,
> considering us no more than brutes? [18:2–3].

Job must think before he speaks; to the friends this means concretely that he
must accept the theology they represent and have been explaining to him in
order to help him. But Job likewise feels sure, not of a doctrine but of his own
experience of life. However much he roots around in his conscience and his
past life, he cannot find a sin that deserves the terrible sufferings he is enduring.
To one so convinced, the friends' arguments seem to lack substance. There is
something out of kilter in the doctrine being expounded to him.

Job is trying to understand how God is just to one who is suffering; he therefore refuses to don the straitjacket of the theology set before him. His friends do not accept this rejection. "Can God deflect the course of right or Shaddai falsify justice?" (8:3), asks Bildad in inquisitorial tones. No, this is how God willed it to be, and there is no room for a view different from the one he is familiar with and has systematically explained in his speech. Seeking is out of place when one is faced with the self-evident. According to Eliphaz, the teaching of the three friends is traditional; it is "the tradition of the sages who have remained faithful to their ancestors" (15:18)—namely, that the wicked live tormented lives, but the upright are rewarded with happiness and plenty.

Job is familiar with this interpretation, which can in fact appeal to themes found in the psalms and sapiential literature of the Bible; but his current experience has undermined his former conviction. Over against the abstract theology of his friends he sets his own experience (and, as we shall see later on, the experience of others, especially the poor). On the basis of this experience, and motivated by the faith he has received from his forebears, he is trying to understand the action of God. He refuses to believe that the love his Lord has for him must necessarily follow the course outlined in the teaching that his friends have been setting before him with such arrogant assurance, perhaps because they are afraid of being left defenseless in the face of life if this teaching should collapse.

Amid his confusion (and despite the response of his friends who accuse him of blaspheming, of speaking ill of God), amid his poverty and suffering, and even though he feels wounded and persecuted by "the hand of God," Job is trying to understand. In their indictments his friends monotonously repeat the same arguments through the several series of speeches. The author of the book may be trying to tell us by this wearisome repetition (which contrasts with the development of Job's thinking) that their theology is an exhausted mine and that it keeps turning in place like a serpent biting its own tail. The only thing that changes in their speeches is the tone, which becomes steadily more hostile and intolerant.

Set against Job's experience, all this seems hollow to him. He is fed up with them and says:

> How often have I heard all this before!
>   What sorry comforters you are!
> "When will these windy arguments be over?"
>   or again, "What sickness drives you to defend
>   yourself?"
> Oh yes! I too could talk as you do,
>   if you were in my place:
>   I could overwhelm you with speeches,
>   shaking my head over you,
> and speak words of encouragement,
>   and then have no more to say.

When I speak, my suffering does not stop;
if I say nothing, is it in any way reduced? [16:2–6].

This is a key passage. It is a rejection of a way of theologizing that does not take account of concrete situations, of the sufferings and hopes of human beings. At the same time, it forgets the gratuitous love and unbounded compassion of God. The friends' speeches are familiar and always the same; they contribute nothing. They have no bearing on Job's experience and suffering; therefore the men who teach in this manner cannot but be "sorry comforters" (in 13:4 he had called them "worthless doctors").[11] The description hits home because his friends' motive in addressing Job is to comfort him.

Eliphaz refers to this when he says, in the speech to which Job is here responding: "Can you ignore these divine consolations and the moderate tone of our words?" (15:11). He is convinced that his arguments should bring relief to Job. He does not see that the inappropriateness of his teaching (in this case its lack of connection with reality) disqualifies it and only makes Job's situation even more unbearable, for it sounds to him like mockery and lies. A little earlier, Job has asked his friends: "Do you mean to defend God by prevarication and by dishonest argument?" (13:7). The question is on the mark and expresses what Job thinks of his friends' theology. The "all this" that he has heard from them does not represent the God whom his faith and suffering make known to him.

Job has launched a cutting, indeed devastating, attack and will not slacken it from here on. How long will his friends go on arguing without ever touching solid ground? What inspires them to continue their "windy arguments"? This phrase of Job is doubtless a rejoinder to what Eliphaz had said in the preceding chapter: "Does anyone wise respond with windy arguments, or feed on an east wind?" (15:2). Later on, the author will ironically have Elihu say that a wind compels him to speak: "I am full of words and forced to speak by a spirit [literally: a wind] within me" (32:18).

His friends' arguments are like a wheel spinning in air: they do not go anywhere. Theirs is the wasted energy of intellectuals who get excited but do not actually do anything; they are incapable of taking a forward step, because the impulse that makes them string arguments together is purely verbal. Why do they keep arguing, Job will ask (and with him all the innocent sufferers in every age of human history), if they have nothing to say? The question applies to every theology that lacks a sense of the mystery of God. The self-sufficient talk of these men is the real blasphemy: their words veil and disfigure the face of a God who loves freely and gratuitously. The friends believe in their theology rather than in the God of their theology.

Job is now in full spate. He mocks these composers of well-ordered speeches. "I too could talk as you do, if you were in my place" (16:4).[12] The friends talk as they do because they have not experienced the abandonment, poverty, and pain that Job has. He tells them sarcastically: "I understand what you say: I would have said the same!" In other words, the dividing line is drawn by personal experience, which sometimes brings a painfully acquired closeness to God, which these untouched theologians with their arguments do not know. That is why they can go on stringing together words, but not ideas, and mocking their addressee with pretended shows of sympathy (that is what "shaking the head" signified in the custom of the time). With renewed irony Job says that their encouragement is simply lip service. Their words are useless and only increase the suffering of the hearer. The suffering does not cease whether they speak or whether they remain silent.

The language we use depends on the situation we are in. Job's words are a criticism of every theology that lacks human compassion and contact with reality; the one-directional movement from theological principles to life really goes nowhere. A quest for understanding that is based on human and religious experience gives a glimpse of other ways of speaking (and keeping silent) about God. Job's sarcasms cannot, however, conceal the fact that he is, as it were, caught in the middle between, on the one side, a theory from which he cannot manage to free himself (the ethico-religious doctrine of retribution) and, on the other, the personal experience that convinces him of his innocence. Despite this dilemma, Job does not let himself be carried away by an abstract and facile logic: he will never say that God is unjust. Instead of speaking ill of the God in whom he believes, he challenges the foundations of the prevailing theology. In this critical attack the faith he has received and his present experience lend support to each other.

His friends try to corner him by claiming that his declaration of innocence amounts to a condemnation of God. Job, put on the defensive, answers that God is not to be justified by condemning the innocent. But the dilemma torments him, and he tries to escape its grip. He does not know how to do it, but he is convinced that the theological method of his friends leads nowhere but to contempt for human beings and thus to a distorted understanding of God. The question remains: How is he to speak of God in the context of his unmerited suffering? That, after all, is the real question: how to speak of God. Job is unyielding in his determination to understand the action of God in history and in his intention of theologizing in the way required by his faith and hope. His course is not clear to him, but at least a trail has been blazed that will permit theologians not to become "worthless doctors" and "sorry comforters" of those who are suffering. He will have to penetrate more deeply into the experience of suffering humanity and into his own experience of God.[13]

CHAPTER 5

The Suffering of Others

The dialogue of Job and his friends advances at an uneven pace, but it does advance. The friends repeat themselves and become increasingly aggressive, but Job sees more deeply into his own experience and refines his thinking. An important point is reached in this progress when he realizes that he is not the only one to experience the pain of unjust suffering. The poor of this world are in the same boat as he: instead of living, they die by the roadside, deprived of the land that was meant to support them. Job discovers to his grief that he has many counterparts in adversity.[1]

The question he asks of God ceases to be a purely personal one and takes concrete form in the suffering of the poor of this world. The answer he seeks will not come except through commitment to them and by following the road—which God alone knows—that leads to wisdom. Job begins to free himself from an ethic centered on personal rewards and to pass to another focused on the needs of one's neighbor. The change represents a considerable shift.

THE LOT OF THE POOR

As his friends continue to insist on the doctrine of temporal retribution, Job ceases to look only at his individual case and asks why it is that the wicked prosper. This first enlargement of the field of experience will supply him with a further argument in the debate with his friends. He will have a new vantage point from which to show the weakness of the arguments brought against him:

> I myself am appalled at the very thought,
>   and my flesh creeps.
> Why do the wicked still live on,
>   their power increasing with their age?
> They see their posterity assured,
>   and their offspring secure before their eyes.
> The peace of their houses has nothing to fear,
>   the rod that God wields is not for them [21:6–9].

"At the very thought": Job is here recalling a fact of daily life, which anyone can verify. The wicked prosper—that is, the very persons who neither serve God nor pray to God:

> They end their lives in happiness
>   and go down in peace to Sheol.
> Yet these are the ones who say to God, "Go away!
>   We do not want to learn your ways.
> What is the point of our serving Shaddai?
>   What should we gain from praying to him? . . ."
> Do we often see the light of the wicked put out,
>   or disaster overtake him,
>   or the retribution of God destroy his possessions,
> or the wind blow him away like a straw,
>   or a whirlwind carrying him off like chaff?
>   [21:13–15, 17–18].

These cases show that the arguments of Job's friends in support of the theory of temporal retribution are in fact worthless; they also show the inadequacy of his friends' references to experience. Job therefore says to them: "So what sense is there in your empty consolation? Your answers are the leftovers of infidelity!" (21:34). The answers do not reflect reality. Job's own experience gives them the lie; furthermore, Job now sees that the question being debated does not concern him alone. This realization gives new vigor to the protest of supposedly "patient" Job, who asks in challenge and complaint: "So God is storing up punishment for his children?" (21:19).

The lot of the wicked is also what leads to the crisis of faith expressed in Psalm 73, a document that is especially close in content to the Book of Job. I shall come back to it later.

Job will reflect more fully on this phenomenon and thus be able to broaden his personal experience still further. As a result, he will distance himself even more quickly and fully from the ethico-religious language of his friends. Moreover, his line of argument will now change radically, as a result precisely of his realization that poverty and abandonment are not his lot alone. For he sees now that this poverty and abandonment are not something fated but are caused by the wicked, who nonetheless live serene and satisfied lives. These are the same ones who tell the Lord, "Go away!" The wicked are both rejecters of God and enemies of the poor—two sides of the one coin. All this leads the author of the book to put into the mouth of Job the most radical and cruel description of the wretchedness of the poor that is to be found in the Bible, and also to have Job utter a harsh indictment of the powerful who rob and oppress the poor.[2]

I think it worthwhile to reproduce in its entirety this passage that is so evidently inspired by the prophets:

The wicked move boundary-marks away,
    they carry off flock and shepherd.
They drive away the orphan's donkey,
    as security, they seize the widow's ox.
The needy have to keep out of the way,
    poor country people have to keep out of sight.
Like wild desert donkeys, they go out to work,
    searching from dawn for food,
    and at evening for something on which to feed their
        children.
They go harvesting in the field of some scoundrel,
    they go pilfering in the vineyards of the wicked.
They go about naked, lacking clothes,
    and starving while they carry the sheaves.
Two little walls, their shelter at high noon;
    parched with thirst, they have to tread the winepress.
They spend the night naked, lacking clothes,
    with no covering against the cold.
Mountain rainstorms cut them through,
    unsheltered, they hug the rocks.
The orphan child is torn from the breast,
    the child of the poor is exacted as security.
From the towns come the groans of the dying
    and the gasp of the wounded crying for help.
    Yet God remains deaf to prayer!
In contrast, there are those who reject the light:
    who know nothing of its ways
    and who do not frequent its paths.
When all is dark the murderer leaves his bed
    to kill the poor and needy.
During the night the thief goes on the prowl,
    breaking into houses while the darkness lasts
                 [24:2–14].

The description is full of detail and shows careful attention to the concrete situation of the poor. The poverty described is not the result of destiny or inexplicable causes; those responsible for it are named without pity. Job is describing a state of affairs caused by the wickedness of those who exploit and rob the poor.[3] In many instances, therefore, the suffering of the innocent points clearly to guilty parties. The daily life of the poor is a dying, says the Bible. The oppressors of the poor are therefore called murderers. The Book of Ecclesiasticus says it bluntly: "The bread of the needy is the life of the poor; whoever deprives them of it is a man of blood. To take away a neighbor's living is to murder him; to deprive an employee of his wages is to shed blood" (34:21–22; see Jer. 22:13–17; Amos 5:11–12; Mic. 2:9–10).

The injustice is even more scandalous because the poor who lack everything and suffer hunger and thirst are the very ones who work to produce for others the food they cannot have for themselves. There is no respect for their basic right to life, though this is the foundation of all justice.[4] With this situation in mind the prophet promises, in words that recall this contrasting passage in Job, that on the day when Yahweh creates new heavens and a new earth "no more shall there be . . . an infant that lives but a few days, or an old man who does not fill out his days. . . . They shall build houses and inhabit them; they shall plant vineyards and eat their fruit. They shall not build and another inhabit; they shall not plant and another eat" (Isa. 65:20–22). This is God's promise of *life,* and it should even now begin to transform the situation of *death* in which the poor live.

The oppressors who kill the poor (the orphan, the widow, the unpaid worker) do their deeds at night, hoping perhaps that the darkness will hide their crimes. But God takes up the cause of the poor. Job realizes that his own situation is that of the poor. Where, then, is God in the midst of it all? Will God be deaf to the prayer of the poor?[5] This time, Job's cry is not simply for himself, for he knows that he is part of the world of the poor. It is in that setting that he asks his question, and it carries with it the questions of all those whom he has just recognized as his fellows in misfortune.[6]

THE WAY OF THE WICKED

When Zophar, who thinks as always within the framework of the theology of temporal retribution, describes the lot of the wicked, he lists among their faults their behavior to the poor:

> Now he has to vomit up the wealth that he has
>   swallowed,
>   God makes him disgorge it.
> He used to suck vipers' venom,
>   and the tongue of the adder kills him.
> No more will he know the streams of oil
>   or the torrents of honey and cream.
> When he gives back his winnings, his cheerfulness will
>   fade,
>   and the satisfied air he had when business was
>   thriving.
> Since he once destroyed the huts of the poor,
>   plundering houses instead of building them up
> > > > > > > [20:15–19].

Job's theologian friends, who know the biblical tradition, are well aware that it is a serious sin to amass wealth through exploitation of the poor. Such behavior contradicts the very meaning of the people's life in the Promised

Land, which was meant to be the opposite of life in Egypt, the land of oppression and injustice. Mistreatment of the helpless is an offense against God; for that reason (Zophar goes on to say) the gladness of the wicked is transitory:

> Since his avarice could never be satisfied,
> now all his hoarding will not save him;
> since nothing could escape his greed,
> his prosperity will not last [20:20–21].

The attitude of the prophets to the poor thus makes a fleeting appearance in the speeches of Job's friends, but is immediately hobbled, as it were, by the doctrine of temporal retribution.

Eliphaz repeats the doctrine at greater length in his final speech, thus spending his last ammunition. It must be acknowledged that his marksmanship has improved.

He has taken note of the attacks on an abstract theology. Job, in ending his series of answers to his friends, has once again called them to task: "What sense is there in your empty consolation? Your answers are the leftovers of infidelity!" (21:34). Eliphaz responds by making his arguments more pointed. He had earlier spoken of the sinfulness of all human beings (chap. 4) and of sin generally as deserving punishment (chap. 15); now he directly accuses Job of serious sins:

> Do you think he is punishing you for your piety
> and bringing you to justice for that?
> No, for your great wickedness, more likely,
> for your unlimited sins!
> You have exacted unearned pledges from your brothers,
> stripped people naked of their clothes,
> failed to give water to the thirsty
> and refused bread to the hungry;
> handed the land over to a strong man,
> for some favoured person to move in,
> sent widows away empty-handed
> and crushed the arms of orphans [22:4–9].

The details of the list are very significant. The emphasis is not on public worship: Was or was not Job a religious man? Eliphaz takes a clearly prophetic stance and finds fault with Job's behavior vis-à-vis the poor. The position that authentic worship presupposes the practice of love and justice is characteristic of the prophetic tradition. Eliphaz adopts it here as he points out that because Job has not practiced the works of mercy, he has failed both justice and God. That is why he finds himself in his present situation:

> No wonder, then, if snares are all around you,
>> and sudden terror makes you afraid;
> if light has turned to darkness, so that you cannot see,
>> and you have been submerged in the flood
>>>> [22:10–11].

Eliphaz's final speech is thus an assertion of the rights of the poor. A key element in his argument is the assumption—for no evidence is adduced—that Job has been guilty of these sins. In fact, Job vehemently denies it, as we shall see in a moment. But first, Eliphaz continues his indictment:

> You have said, "What does God know?
>> Can he judge through the dark cloud?
> The clouds, to him, are an impenetrable veil,
>> as he goes his way on the rim of the heavens."
> And will you still follow the ancient trail
>> trodden by the wicked . . . ? [22:13–15].

In Eliphaz's view, then, Job behaves like all the other wicked who do not believe that God sees their deeds. This is a typical reproach leveled at evildoers. Eliphaz seems to argue that if Job denies temporal retribution, it can only be because he thinks God is unaware of what goes on among human beings. In fact, then, the prophetic standpoint that Eliphaz has to some extent adopted in this speech has not led him to abandon the doctrine of retribution, which he and his two friends have been so fervently defending. His reasoning, as we have already seen, is this: Job is suffering, therefore he *must* have committed these sins. Job will appeal to facts and reject this argument that is based solely on doctrinal principles and undeterred by any concern to check it against reality.

On the basis of what he has said, Eliphaz urges Job to conversion. His words are fervent and marked by beauty of expression:

> Well then! Make peace with him, be reconciled,
>> and all your happiness will be restored to you.
> Welcome the teaching from his lips,
>> and keep his words close to your heart.
> If you return, humbled, to Shaddai
>> and drive wickedness from your tent,
> if you lay your gold down on the dust,
>> Ophir down among the pebbles of the torrent,
> Shaddai will be bars of gold to you
>> and silver piled in heaps.
> Then Shaddai will be all your delight,
>> and you will lift your face to God.
> You will pray, and he will hear;
>> and you will be able to fulfill your vows.

Whatever you undertake will go well,
>   and light will shine on your path;
for he casts down the pride of the arrogant,
>   but he saves those of downcast eyes.
He rescues anyone who is innocent;
>   have your hands clean, and you will be saved
>   [22:21–30].

The conversion Eliphaz has in mind supposes that Job acknowledges his sin and separates himself from it: "Drive wickedness from your tent." Job is being urged to depart from the "ancient trail" of the wicked (22:15) in order that "light" may shine "on your path" (22:28). Thus the darkness that keeps him from seeing his way will be dispersed (see 3:23). The way (Hebrew, *derek*) of the just is here contrasted with the way of the wicked and refers to the conduct of those who advance toward God by doing God's will. Eliphaz ends with the promise of deliverance: "He rescues anyone who is innocent; have your hands clean [that is, practice justice], and you will be saved."

It must be recognized that within the limits imposed by his theology, Eliphaz has made a great effort to be reconciled with Job. Meanwhile, Job's outlook has been broadened by his realization of the suffering and injustice that are the lot of the poor. Consequently, even when denying the misdeeds of which Eliphaz accuses him, he sees more clearly that if he is to be just he must pay heed to the poor and set them free.

His friend's argument will help Job to launch a very interesting process in which his individual situation becomes less and less the focus of the debate. He will broaden his perspective to include the sufferings and injustices to which the poor fall victim, as we saw in the preceding section of this chapter. This broadening of outlook will in turn enable him to develop the rudiments of a new way of talking about God.

Job's other two friends, Bildad and Zophar, also deliver their final speeches.[7] These amount to repetitive indictments incapable of carrying further the bold attempt made by Eliphaz, who undoubtedly has the sharpest mind of the three. For this reason, they succeed only in angering Job:

I swear by the living God who denies me justice,
>   by Shaddai who has filled me with bitterness,
that as long as a shred of life is left in me,
>   and the breath of God breathes in my nostrils,
my lips will never speak evil
>   nor my tongue utter any lie.
Far from admitting you to be in the right,
>   I shall maintain my integrity to my dying day.
I take my stand on my uprightness, I shall not stir:
>   in my heart I need not be ashamed of my days.
Let my enemy meet the fate of the wicked,
>   my adversary, the lot of the evil-doer! [27:2–7].

The three friends have said what they were able to say; their store of arguments is exhausted. They will not speak again. Disagreeing with them, Job has asserted his integrity and uprightness. His conviction of his innocence has become a solid rock within him. He now solemnly assures them that he will maintain this position to the end of his life. Nothing will persuade him to the contrary. This is a matter of conscience, but of a conscience that is guided by a lofty ideal of truth. Were he to agree with his friends, he would be lying; neither his faith in God nor his state of mind will allow him to do it. He will not fall back on deception in order to ease his situation and achieve a degree of repose. His truthfulness leaves him isolated and almost defenseless. Who is the adversary he has in mind in the last verse of the passage just cited? His friends? God? Someone else? Scholars are in disagreement.

From the legal standpoint that Job several times adopts, the possible guilt of anyone challenging him will be proof of his own innocence. In the verse to which I have just referred, Job is not really accusing anyone; he has his own interests in mind. His words, especially if they refer to God, are harsh; yet, much to his regret, the whole form that the theological debate with his friends has taken down to this point forces him to utter them. He is exhausted, and so is the debate. The road they have been traveling has led into a blind alley; Job has had the courage to follow the road to the end in order to prove that this is where it must lead. Fresh air is needed, and a radical change of perspective.

The author, a poetic genius, will see to it that our legitimate longing for an answer to the questions formulated does not itself remain rudimentary and unmediated. It must mature, penetrate each of us more deeply, and take historical form. The question we face here is not one that can be handled by what Blaise Pascal calls the *esprit géométrique,* or mathematical mind, which reasons in an orderly way from definitions and principles. What is needed is rather the *esprit de finesse,* or intuitive mind, which is capable of a penetrating, comprehensive vision of a reality accessible to all.[8] The poet helps us develop this vision by giving us now a beautiful poem on wisdom (chap. 28) and putting us in the presence (as though in an interval of waiting between the preceding debate and the last and more important speeches of the book) of the greatness of God and the hidden understanding of God's intentions for the human race.[9]

Gently, and in verses of great beauty, the author reminds us that the quest on which Job is bent requires a prudence (discernment) that wisdom alone gives. Possession of this wisdom is identical with fear of the Lord. The poem tells us that human beings know where to find silver, iron, and a great many other things, but that where wisdom is concerned, "God alone understands her path and knows where she is to be found" (28:23). At the same time, he also shows in a subtle way that something new is needed if we are to share in the knowledge of God. Chapter 28 thus serves as a poetic hinge, so to speak, in the development of the book.[10]

CHAPTER 6

God and the Poor

J ob began his part in the debate with a monologue; he now ends it with
another. He continues to defend his integrity, as he had promised. But
because he now has in mind other innocent persons besides himself, his
argument is enriched, and his voice changes pitch, as it were. As he recalls his
past and the demands made by his God, he shows a clear understanding of the
religious meaning of service to the poor.

An unexpected personage will come on the scene: the elusive and boastful
Elihu. Despite everything—despite himself—he has something new to say,
certain nuances to contribute. He picks up the thread of the debate, dis-
tinguishes himself from those who have played a part in it thus far, and helps
broaden the horizon within which the final dialogue between God and the most
upright of human beings will unfold.

TO FREE THE POOR

In a lengthy monologue (chaps. 29–31) that to some extent parallels the
opening monologue in chapter 3, Job makes a solemn statement (29:1) as he
looks back over his life. He allows himself the time to do it properly. He is no
longer debating those foolish theologians, his friends, but is talking now to
himself or perhaps to a wider public and doing so in a more mature way. The
monologue is a kind of testimony about his life, a plea in the trial he has several
times asked for. He has not forgotten Eliphaz's last accusation, however; it has
led him to understand that innocence is not a matter simply of individual
uprightness. It is rather a question above all of one's behavior to the poor, who
are especially loved by the Lord.

Job looks back nostalgically to "the days when God was my guardian"
(29:2) and his life was filled with happiness. He also remembers how he acted at
that time:

> I freed the poor in distress
> and the orphan who had no helper.

39

> The dying man's blessing rested on me,
>   and I gave the widow's heart cause to rejoice.
> Uprightness I wore as a garment,
>   fair judgement was my cloak and my turban.
> I was eyes for the blind
>   and feet for the lame.
> Who but me was father of the poor?
>   The stranger's case had a hearing from me.
> I used to break the fangs of the wicked
>   and snatch their prey from their jaws [29:12–17].

Uprightness or "justice" (*ṣedaqāh*) and judgment (*mishpaṭ*) are two key words in the Bible. The practice of them is one of the great biblical commandments (see Gen. 18:19), because they are a task to which God is committed.[1] Job has made their practice a permanent part of his life ("my cloak and my turban"). Uprightness and judgment cannot be promoted in the abstract but only in relation to the inhuman situation in which orphans, widows, and strangers live ("orphans, widows, and strangers" is a classical biblical synonym for "the poor"). "Father of the poor" (v. 16) is one of God's titles: "Father of the fatherless and protector of widows is God in his holy habitation" (Ps. 68:5). The behavior required of those who want to be faithful to the Lord is: "Be like a father to orphans" (Ecclus. 4:10; see also Isa. 22:21).[2] And it must be remembered that this commitment implies resistance to oppressors and evildoers (see Ps. 3:7; 58:6; 101:8).[3]

The obligation to care for the poor means that the poor are not persons being punished by God (as the doctrine of temporal retribution implicitly asserts), but rather God's friends. To give to the needy is therefore to give to God: "He who is kind to the poor lends to the Lord" (Prov. 19:17); and, conversely, "He who oppresses a poor man insults his Maker" (Prov. 14:31; see 17:5). The full implications of this attitude and the full extent of the obligation it imposes will be revealed when Christ identifies himself with the poor of this world (see Matt. 25:31–46).

The image of a "father" that the Bible uses in this connection brings out the close and affectionate relationship that should characterize this commitment to the poor. But the image also implies determination: defense of the poor requires their liberation ("I freed the poor," v. 12) and resistance to those who oppress and exploit them ("I used to break the fangs of the wicked, and snatch their prey from their jaws," v. 17).

Job's life bears witness to his solidarity with the poor and the helpless:

> Yet have I ever laid a hand on the poor
>   when they cried out for justice in calamity?
> Have I not wept for those whose life is hard,
>   felt pity for the penniless? [30:24–25].[4]

These verses resemble 29:12–17 but they add a complaint of Job to God. Job has asked for justice and not been heard; yet he himself has heeded the cry of the poor. He says, therefore, in sad disillusionment: "I hoped for happiness, but sorrow came; I looked for light, but there was darkness" (30:26).

In the monologue Job is giving his answer to Eliphaz, whose accusations were the work of his own imagination. "Contempt for the poor" is not a true description of Job's past behavior. On the contrary, he can boast of having done works of mercy and thereby practiced an uprightness beyond that required by the law. Consequently, he has not offered dishonest sacrifices to God or tried to bribe God with a worship lacking in love for the poor who are God's beloved. Job has in fact always been responsive to the warning in Ecclesiasticus:

> Do not offer him a bribe, for he will not accept it;
>> and do not trust to an unrighteous sacrifice;
> for the Lord is the judge
>> and with him there is no partiality.
> He will not show partiality in the case of a poor man;
>> and he will listen to the prayer of one who is
>>> wronged.
> He will not ignore the supplications of the fatherless,
>> nor the widow when she pours out her story
>>> [35:12–14].

But then the question inevitably arises: If Job's suffering is not the result of a sinful life, in what sense is God just? Job is convinced of his own innocence and claims that he has always respected the rights of the poorest. This leads him in turn to a solemn declaration of the equality of all human beings before God:[5]

> If I have ever infringed the rights of slave
>> or slave-girl in legal actions against me—
> what shall I do, when God stands up?
>> What shall I say when he holds his assize?
> Did he not create them in the womb like me,
>> the same God forming us in the womb? [31:13–15].

This passage resembles one in the prophet Malachi that makes the universal fatherhood of God the basis for the ethical requirements of the covenant: "Have we not all one father? Has not one God created us? Why, then, are we faithless to one another, profaning the covenant of our fathers?" (2:10).[6]

Job continues his challenge as he recalls, in a series of questions, the ways in which he has committed himself to the poor:

> Have I been insensible to the needs of the poor,
>> or let a widow's eyes grow dim?

> Have I eaten my bit of bread on my own
> > without sharing it with the orphan?
> For from childhood the orphan has grown up close to
> > me,
> > and from his mother's womb I have guided him.[7]
> Have I ever seen a wretch in need of clothing,
> > or the poor with nothing to wear,
> without his having cause to bless me from his heart,
> > as he felt the warmth of the fleece from my lambs?
> Have I raised my hand against an orphan
> > presuming on my credit at the gate?
> If so, let my shoulder fall from its socket,
> > let my arm break off at the elbow! [31:16–22].

Job is sure that he has acted properly, and he indicates in detail the ways in which he has acted: attention to the needs of the poor, counsel for the afflicted, food for the hungry, guidance for the orphan, clothing and shelter for the destitute, justice for the innocent. We find similar lists of the works of mercy in other parts of the Bible; they prescribe how believers in the God of the covenant are to behave.[8] Job has made them the standard for his own life, and the accusation made against him by Eliphaz (chap. 22) is seen to have no basis in fact. More than that, he has shared his table with the poor, and not just as an occasional gesture inspired by transitory feeling. He has always remained close to the orphaned ("from his mother's womb," he says in a hyperbole, v. 18) and tried to be a father to them (same thought in 29:16, "Who but me was father of the poor?").

Not only did Job deal justly with the poor; he also practiced a kind of ecological justice toward the earth, mother of life and source of food for the poor. Before the bar of the earth and those who work it, he is no less innocent than in his dealings with the poor:

> If my land cries for vengeance against me
> > and its furrows weep in concert,
> if I have eaten its produce without paying,
> > and caused the death of owners [or: workers],
> let brambles grow instead of wheat,
> > rank weeds instead of barley! [31:38–40].

Job, then, sees himself as father of the poor and enemy of those who seek to devour them. He regards himself as upright because he has cultivated a neighborly solidarity with the oppressed and dispossessed: "Have I not wept for those whose life is hard, felt pity for the penniless? . . . No stranger ever had to sleep outside, my door was always open to the traveler" (30:25; 31:32). The establishment of "uprightness and judgment" requires that the poor be freed from the inhuman situation of exploitation in which they live. This effort—Job now sees clearly—defines the innocence, before God and other human beings, that he has claimed for himself throughout the debate with his friends.[9]

It is significant that Job connects his commitment to the poor with another central theme of the Bible—the rejection of idolatry. After recalling how he has dealt with the helpless, he says:

> Have I put faith in gold,
>   saying to fine gold, "Ah, my security"?
> Have I ever gloated over my great wealth,
>   or the riches that my hands have won?
> Or has the sight of the sun in its glory,
>   or the glow of the moon as it walked the sky,
> secretly stolen my heart,
>   so that I blew them a kiss?
> That too would be a criminal offence,
>   to have denied the supreme God [31:24–28].

He was not a covetous man, or an idolater as St. Paul would say.[10] Money was not his god, nor did he let his life depend on it,[11] just as he did not entrust that life to the care of sun or moon. That would have been to deny "the supreme God." On the contrary, he wanted his life to be one of surrender to the God who has a preferential love of the poor. Therefore he tried to be attentive to the needs of the poor.[12] It is in this surrender that his innocence consists. But then, once again, why is he subjected to unjust suffering? "Will no one give me a hearing?" he exclaims just before the end of his final speech.

DIVINE PEDAGOGY AND THE CRY OF THE OPPRESSED

Everything suggests that God will at last speak out. Job has persistently called upon God to put in an appearance.[13] God still does not do so, but, surprisingly, someone named Elihu does come on the scene.[14] There has been no indication that such a person has been present during Job's debate with his friends. The prologue says nothing of him, and neither will the epilogue.[15] Until now he has been satisfied to listen to what his elders have to say. Like all young men in the traditional societies (we need think only of the peasant world in the mountainous regions of Peru), he has not dared to speak up; in his short life he has not yet acquired the experience needed, if he is to intervene. Now, however, he decides to break his respectful silence, because the lengthy debate to which he has been listening has been deeply disappointing to him. He begins:

> I am still young,
>   and you are old,
> so I was shy and hesitant
>   to tell you what I know.

> I thought, "Age ought to speak,
> > advancing years will convey wisdom."
> There is, you see, a spirit residing in humanity,
> > the breath of God conferring intelligence.
> Great age does not give wisdom,
> > nor seniority fair judgement [32:6–9].

Elihu is persuaded that he has something worth saying in response to Job's self-justifications and in view of Job's friends' inability to answer them ("none of you has confounded Job, not one of you has refuted what he says," 32:12). All that he has heard has made him realize that God alone, and not ripe years, gives understanding of things. Elihu therefore decides to speak; he thinks of himself as inspired and that is how he presents himself (v. 18).[16] He is no friend of Job, and his words will therefore be cold and distant. His purpose, unlike the original purpose of Eliphaz and his companions, is not to comfort, but to teach and pass judgment:

> Now I shall have my say,
> > my turn has come to say what I know.
> For I am full of words
> > and forced to speak by a spirit within me;
> within me, it feels like new wine seeking a vent,
> > bursting out of new wine-skins.
> To gain relief, I must speak,
> > I must open my lips and reply [32:17–20].[17]

Elihu moves to the personal level and issues his challenge directly to Job, whom he several times calls by name. He speaks with some arrogance, as a man very sure of his views. He does not take into account Job's situation or suffering; nor does he enter into Job's harsh experiences or agonizing questions. His thoughts run along other lines, and his purpose is other than Job's— it is to defend what he considers to be correct teaching:

> Pay attention, Job, listen to me;
> > keep quiet, I have more to say.
> If you have anything to say, refute me,
> > speak out, for I would gladly accept that you are
> > > upright.
> If not, then listen to me:
> > keep quiet, and I will teach you wisdom [33:31–33].

Though conceited, Elihu has a good grasp of what has been said in the debate and is thus able to focus on important points. The young theologian first recalls the greatness of God (he will later dwell on this at length). With this as his starting point, he is able to give a complete and flexible version of the doctrine of temporal retribution. He does not reject this doctrine, and there-fore can say to Job: "He pays people back for what they do, treating each as his own conduct deserves. Be sure of it: God never does wrong, Shaddai does not pervert what is just" (34:11–12). Elihu does, however, distance himself to some degree from Job's friends; his position is more nuanced and even novel. He recalls Job's posture as accuser of God and is indignant at him for it. In his usual pompous way he says:

> How could you say in my hearing—
>   for the sound of your words did not escape me—
> "I am clean, and sinless,
>   I am pure, without fault.
> But he keeps inventing excuses against me
>   and regards me as his enemy.
> He puts me in the stocks,
>   he watches my every path"?
> In saying so, I tell you, you are wrong:
>   for God is greater than any human being [33:8–12].

"God is greater than any human being": Elihu is deeply convinced of this, and it is, as I said above, one of his main themes. Job's boldness is due to his not realizing the place that adversity may have in God's plans. This is a subtle and many-sided matter. The point Elihu wants to concentrate on is not so much the source and cause of suffering, but the why of it, its finality in divine prov-idence. The ways of God are not easy to understand and will be even less easy for those who use the simplistic categories of Job and his friends:

> God speaks first in one way,
>   and then in another, although we do not realize it.
> In dreams and in night-visions,
>   when slumber has settled on humanity
>   and people are asleep in bed,
> he speaks in someone's ear,
>   frightens him with apparitions
> to turn him from what he is doing
>   and to put an end to his pride.
> And thus he preserves his soul from the abyss,
>   his life from passing down the Canal.
> Or again, he corrects by the sufferings of the sick-bed,
>   when someone's bones tremble continuously
> and the thought of food revolts him,
>   however tasty it is [33:14–20].

Elihu's contribution to the debate is important and very much his own. God uses different modes of self-manifestation, and suffering can be one of them

(Eliphaz had earlier suggested this theme: 5:17–18). In view of Job's impatience, Elihu warns him of the danger of being deaf to God. Attention is needed, for God may speak in unexpected ways. Misfortune is not always a punishment, as the friends and even Job himself suppose; it can also have a pedagogical purpose.[18] Job has been complaining that God does not speak to him; Elihu answers that suffering can contain a revelation of God. Further on, this recent arrival on the scene returns to the point and, speaking of God, says: "God saves the afflicted by his affliction, warning him in his misery" (36:15). Suffering disposes one to hear and accept the word of God.

This explanation does not do away with the mystery of suffering in human life. The poet is using Elihu to convey one answer given in his day[19] to the difficulty that the doctrine of retribution is at odds with human experience. It is clear, however, that the author is not satisfied with this answer; the best of his own thinking will be given in the speeches of God from the heart of the tempest.

For the moment Elihu urges Job to change his attitude. This whole business must end in a conversion to God: "He will pray to God, and God will hear him and show his face joyfully to him; and he will give him back his salvation" (33:26).[20] The assertion of the pedagogical value of suffering thus has for its context a theme that, as I said earlier, is especially dear to this impetuous speaker: the greatness of God. He will return to it in chapters 36 and 37 with a spate of talk that seems, at first sight, to anticipate the speeches of God. It should be noted that Job too speaks of this theme on several occasions.

According to Elihu, the suit that Job is trying to bring against God is absurd and disrespectful: "It is not for a human being to appoint a time for appearing in court with God" (34:23).[21] His speeches show he does not believe that God will agree to Job's plea and challenge: God will not come and speak to Job; God is too great for that. Furthermore, Elihu, this young and self-satisfied theologian, thinks that in the speeches he has addressed to Job, Job has all the thoughts he needs to calm his anxiety.

There is a second point Elihu emphasizes—namely, the attitude of God to the poor. Here he adopts a prophetic style of discourse about God. In continuity with the entire tradition of Israel, he will eventually say that God "does accord fair judgement to the afflicted" (36:6).

He begins by reminding his listener that in God's eyes all human beings are equal. This is a basic characteristic of divine justice. God "is unimpressed by princes and makes no distinction between rich and poor, since all alike have been made by him" (34:19).

If God does make distinctions, it is in favor of the most helpless, those who are oppressed by the mighty:

> He breaks the powerful without inquiry
>   and sets up others in their places.
> He knows the sort of things they do!
>   He overthrows them at night, to be trampled on.

> He beats them like criminals,
>   chained up for all to see,
> since they have turned their backs on him,
>   having understood so little of his ways
> as to make the cries of the weak rise to him
>   and let him hear the appeal of the afflicted
>   [34:24–28].

Job has already received insight into the role of commitment to the poor in obtaining true justice and as a requirement of God. Elihu now predicates this behavior of God. He does it in a somewhat formal way, it is true, and without completely abandoning the doctrine of retribution. His emphasis on the point is nonetheless a continuation of what has been said in the debate. God does justice to the poor; that is why those who oppress the poor turn their backs on God and understand so little of God's ways—that is, of the conduct that God requires of believers. Mistreatment of the poor causes them to cry out to God, and their cry is heard. The reference to the paradigmatic experience of the exodus is clear ("I . . . have heard their cry because of their taskmasters"—Exod. 3:7).

This relationship of God and the poor is the very heart of the prophetic message. The Lord is ever watchful and ready to hear the voice of the poor, even though attentiveness to them may at times take unobtrusive forms. Job has allowed himself to doubt this concern on God's part, and Elihu therefore reprimands him:

> But if he is silent, who can condemn him?
>   If he hides his face, who can see him?
> He is watching over nations and individuals
>   so that the wicked will not reign
>   and there be none to deceive the people [34:29–30].[22]

Elihu seems to think he has said the last word in the debate but this will not be the case. In fact, as I mentioned earlier, he himself will not be mentioned again in the book. But his part in the debate—in which key elements are still lacking—has prepared us to listen to Yahweh. This is due both to what the young theologian has had to say and to the tremendous lacunae in his speeches.[23]

Let me summarize quickly what has been said in the second part of this book, which has described a milestone in Job's effort to learn how to speak of God. Job began by talking of his suffering and then of the injustice he saw in his individual lot. His point of departure was both his own experience and his faith in the living God; it was on that basis that he challenged, and gradually dismantled, the doctrine of retribution that his three friends expounded in a pompous and abstract manner, and that Elihu was subsequently to explain more intelligently.

The dialogue has, however, led Job to broaden his vision. A shift pregnant with consequences has taken place. Job now reflects on the situation of others—namely, the poor, and their undeserved suffering. "Yet God remains deaf to prayer!" (24:12), he wonders as he raises this key issue. Going more deeply into this matter of the poor, he recalls the great requirements of the covenant (without mentioning the covenant by name): real belief in God entails solidarity with the poor so as to ease their undeserved suffering by establishing "uprightness and judgment."[24] This is a major theme in the prophetic tradition of Israel.

Job next calls to mind his own actions in this area. By means of them he had been able to speak of God. Now that he is sharing the lot of the poor in his own flesh, his talk of God becomes more profound and truthful. The point is that commitment to the poor provides firm ground for prophetic talk of God. The prophets repeatedly stress the importance of fidelity to the covenant. When they deal so sternly with the sins of their people, they are speaking *in place of* God (that is what *nabi,* the Hebrew word for "prophet," means). At the same time, in their discourses they talk primarily *about* God.

Their language has its historical roots in commitment to the poor, who are the favorites of God. In that context aspects of God's nature hidden in other approaches to God come to light. At the same time God makes new demands on human behavior: as Proverbs says, "he who mocks the poor insults his Maker" (17:5). God is the ultimate and comprehensive ground of human behavior. This is the central idea in the ethic of the reign of God, the proclamation of which becomes more and more definite as the Bible advances, reaching its full form in Jesus the Messiah.

This realization, which is partially attained by Elihu, gives Job a way of talking about God on the basis of his experience of suffering and injustice. To go out of himself and help other sufferers (without waiting until his own problems are first resolved) is to find a way to God. The reason for his own unjust situation is a question that still gnaws at him, but he now begins to see that he may not let it be an obstacle to immediate commitment to the poor. The needs of others cannot be left in abeyance until everything has become clear.[25]

In addition, solidarity with the marginalized and suffering of this world adds weight to Job's demand for an explanation of the relationship between a just God and the suffering of the innocent. Above all, however, Job sees that commitment to the poor puts everything on a solid basis, a basis located outside his individual world, in the needs of others who cannot be ignored. All this constitutes the beginning of an answer to his questions. That is, it is a step on the way to correct talk of God: a God who, as Job knows in the depths of his heart, wants justice. That is why Job can believe that in practicing justice he is doing the will of God.

But this kind of talk about God—talk that may be described as "prophetic"—is inadequate. Job's thirst for understanding, which his trials have awakened and inflamed, is not satisfied. Gropingly, and resisting false images, he looks insatiably for a deeper insight into divine justice and an unlimited encounter with the God in whom he believes and hopes.

PART 3

The Language of Contemplation

How are we to talk to God in view of the suffering of the innocent? This is the central question in the Book of Job. The linking of God and the poor has opened up a way of answering the question. Commitment to those most forgotten is a requirement of the God of the Bible, but this fact need not be completely clear for one to see the urgency of the requirement and put it into practice. Commitment is a first expression of that disinterested faith on which the satan cast doubt at the threshold of Job's speeches. Commitment to the poor gives rise to a way of talking about God that influences the concrete behavior of believers. They thus retain the ethical perspective that is part of the theology of retribution, but they now situate it in a new and different context.

Converging with this prophetic line of thought about God is another that initially appears rather unobtrusively but in the end takes an almost explosive form—the line embodied in the language of mysticism. Its first expression, both simple and profound, is at the level of the faith of the people.

CHAPTER 7

Everything Comes from God

When misfortune befalls him, Job's first and spontaneous reaction is one of acceptance and trust in God. Grieved, but with undiminished conviction, he exclaims:

> Naked I came from my mother's womb,
>   naked I shall return again.
> Yahweh gave, Yahweh has taken back.
> Blessed be the name of Yahweh! [1:21].

These well-known and often cited verses are doubtless the reason why Job is so frequently described as "patient." Instead of *cursing* God, as the satan claimed he would, Job *blesses* the name of the Lord. The narrator can justifiably say that "in all this misfortune Job committed no sin, and he did not reproach God" (1:22).

The second testing, in which sickness is added to poverty, does not make Job change his views. Seated "among the ashes" and plagued by misfortune, he nevertheless refuses to follow the advice of his infuriated wife who rebukes him: "Why persist in this integrity of yours? Curse God and die" (2:9). The satan's outlook seems to have found an echo among those who are close to Job and share his suffering. But he answers steadfastly: "That is how a fool of a woman talks. If we take happiness from God's hand, must we not take sorrow too?" (2:10). It is the same answer that he gave to the first onslaught of the satan: acceptance of the will of God.

This passage again ends with a statement by the author of the book: "And in all this misfortune Job uttered no sinful word" (2:10). That is, Job did not speak ill of God despite his impoverishment, his loneliness, and his sufferings; on the contrary, he showed a profound sense of the gratuitousness of God's love. Everything comes from God and is God's gracious gift; no human being, therefore, has a right to make any demands. Contrary to what the satan has claimed, Job's religion is indeed disinterested—that is, given freely, "for nothing." He does not need material prosperity to sustain his trust in God. After

53

each trial Job is said to "persist in his integrity." This persistence shows that his faith and behavior are not inspired by hope of material reward. It is thus made clear from the outset that gratuitousness is a main characteristic of authentic faith in God. The book will end on the same note.

The language used by Job in these opening chapters is often found on the lips of the poor who are believers. How often we hear simple folk use the very words of Job at the loss of loved ones: "God gave them to me, God has taken them away from me." This faith is sometimes described as "the faith of a cleaning lady," but this seems inaccurate. There is something deeper here, something that more learned types find difficult to grasp. The faith of the people is characterized by a strong sense of the lordship of God. It has a spontaneous understanding of what Yahweh says in Leviticus: "The land shall not be sold in perpetuity, for the land is mine; for you are strangers and sojourners with me" (25:23). The believing people is deeply convinced that everything belongs to the Lord and comes from the Lord.[1] This conviction is well expressed in the beautiful prayer of David: "All things come from thee, and of thy own have we given thee. For we are strangers before thee, and sojourners, as all our fathers were" (1 Chron. 29:14-15).

Job's language here is, in outline, the language of contemplation and contains all its values. At the same time, however, his language shares the limitations of the faith of the poor; if one remains at this level, one cannot withstand the onslaught of ideologized ways of talking about God. That is, the faith of simple folk can be manipulated by interpretations alien to their religious experience. Furthermore, as happens in Job's own case, unremitting poverty and suffering give rise to difficult questions. A quick acceptance of them can signify a resignation to evil and injustice that will later be an obstacle to faith in the God who liberates. The insights present in the faith of the people must therefore be deepened and vitalized, but this process requires certain separations.

In the Book of Job these separations occur when Job's friends try to justify his sufferings. Job then reacts and debates with these theologians, as we saw. But as his vision broadens and deepens, he realizes that the debate is not with them but with God. In the final analysis, the author of the book shows Job's theologian friends talking *about* God but never *to* God, as Job himself does.[2]

Job then begins to call for an explanation from a God who seems to avoid him. His friends are incapable of following him along this path; their theology makes it impossible for them. Subsequently, Job speaks as follows of this painful course:

> My lament is still rebellious;
>   despite my groans, his hand is just as heavy.
> Will no one help me to know
>   how to travel to his dwelling? . . .
> If I go to the east, he is not there;
>   or to the west, I still cannot find him.

If I seek him in the north, he is not to be found,
   invisible as ever, if I turn to the south.
And yet he knows every step I take!
   Let him test me in the crucible: I shall come out pure
      gold.
My footsteps have followed close in his,
   I have walked in his way without swerving;
I have not neglected the commandment of his lips,
   in my heart I have cherished the words of his mouth
                              [23:2–3, 8–12].

This difficult journey will not essentially change Job's recognition that everything comes from God. On the contrary, this conviction will be strengthened and deepened, and will have a new perspective and scope. But the road Job travels will show clearly that his acceptance of God's will is not simply resignation. His full encounter with his God comes by way of complaint, bewilderment, and confrontation.[3]

CHAPTER 8

The Spiritual Struggle

J ob's rebellious attitude is due not so much to his sufferings as to the arguments that his friends develop in their pompous manner. This is clear from his opening monologue (chap. 3), which I discussed earlier; it expresses profound suffering but not the confrontation with God that we find later on. To be more accurate, I would say that a situation that Job considers unjust becomes intolerable when justified by the theological arguments of his three friends. At this point he enters upon a real spiritual struggle with God. The Bible gives us more than than one example of this kind of confrontation; none, however, is so powerful and radical as the one in this book. Job boldly demands that God come forth; that God listen to Job and speak to him. Yet in the final analysis the demand is inspired by a firm trust in God himself.

Three key passages serve to mark a like number of important stages in the spiritual struggle of Job with God in this one-way journey to God that he has undertaken in the name of suffering, hopeful, and bewildered humankind. I refer to 9:33 on the need of an arbiter (Hebrew, *mokhiach*); 16:19 on the presence of an witness (*'ēdh*) to the discussion; and 19:25 on the hope of a defender or liberator (*gō'ēl*). The three roles or functions represent three faces of one and the same God as experienced by one who suffers adversity and is searching.

NEED OF AN ARBITER

The arguments of his friends spur Job to an angry assertion of his innocence. He knows, however, that in a contest with God he must be the loser: "Indeed, I know it is as you say: how could anyone claim to be upright before God?" (9:2). He recognizes that God transcends human beings, but, given the situation he is enduring, the acknowledgment means that he feels trapped. He says as much in the harshest words that the author puts in his mouth:

> Even if I am upright, what point is there in answering
>   him?
> I can only plead for mercy with my judge!

And if he deigned to answer my citation,
    I cannot believe he would listen to what I said,
he who crushes me for one hair,
    who, for no reason, wounds and wounds again,
not even letting me regain my breath,
    with so much bitterness he fills me!
Shall I try force? Look how strong he is!
    Or go to court? But who will summon him?
If I prove myself upright, his mouth may condemn me,
    even if I am innocent, he may pronounce me
        perverse.
But am I innocent? I am no longer sure,
    and life itself I despise!
It is all one, and hence I boldly say:
    he destroys innocent and guilty alike.
When a sudden deadly scourge descends,
    he laughs at the plight of the innocent.
When a country falls into the power of the wicked,
    he veils the face of its judges.
    Or if not he, who else? [9:15–24].

Job seems close here to speaking ill of God. We have reached the tensest moment in his dispute with the Lord. He asserts and repeats his integrity and innocence, but at the same time criticizes the seemingly irrational way in which God acts: "It is all one, and hence I boldly say: he destroys innocent and guilty alike." Job also reproaches God with injustice: "He laughs at the plight of the innocent" and allows a country to "fall into the power of the wicked." In plain language he lets it be known whom he regards as responsible for this situation: "If not he, who else?"

Bold words, these, that have their source in unbearable suffering. And yet such language is not so foreign to the Bible.[1] On various occasions, persons of deep faith bitterly question the way God governs the world. An example of someone in a situation very like that of Job is to be found in Psalm 73, which appears in fact to be one of the sources used by the author of the Book of Job. Here are some verses:

As for me, my feet had almost stumbled,
    my steps had well nigh slipped.
For I was envious of the arrogant,
    when I saw the prosperity of the wicked.
For they have no pangs;
    their bodies are sound and sleek.
They are not in trouble as other men are;
    they are not stricken like other men.

> Therefore pride is their necklace;
>   violence covers them as a garment.
> Their eyes swell out with fatness,
>   their hearts overflow with follies.
> They scoff and speak with malice;
>   loftily they threaten oppression.
> They set their mouths against the heavens,
>   and their tongue struts through the earth.
> Therefore the people turn and praise them;
>   and find no fault in them.
> And they say, "How can God know?
>   Is there knowledge in the Most High?"
> Behold, these are the wicked;
>   always at ease, they increase in riches.
> All in vain have I kept my heart clean
>   and washed my hands in innocence.
> For all day long I have been stricken,
>   and chastened every morning [Ps. 73:2–14].

Another example occurs in the lamentations attributed to Jeremiah:

> I am the man who has seen affliction
>   under the rod of his wrath;
> he has driven and brought me
>   into darkness without any light;
> surely against me he turns his hand
>   again and again the whole day long.
> He has made my flesh and my skin waste away,
>   and broken my bones;
> he has besieged and enveloped me
>   with bitterness and tribulation;
> he has made me dwell in darkness
>   like the dead of long ago.
> He has walled me about so that I cannot escape;
>   he has put heavy chains on me;
> though I call and cry for help,
>   he shuts out my prayer;
> he has blocked my ways with hewn stones,
>   he has made my paths crooked [Lam. 3:1–9].

For the authors of these texts, confrontation with God is a paradoxical way of expressing their faith. They complain to the God in whom they believe. Yet it must be acknowledged that these other passages do not reach the level of daring that Job shows.[2]

Job wants to initiate something resembling a lawsuit with God.[3] Now, if a court is to pass judgment in his confrontation with God, an arbiter will be needed. But where is someone to be found who can mediate between God and himself? Eliphaz had said in his very first speech that such an appeal would be useless and counterproductive:

> Make your appeal then. Will you find an answer?
> To which of the holy ones will you turn?
> Resentment kills the senseless,
> and anger brings death to the fool [5:1–2].

Despite this, Job continues to voice his desire, although somewhat dejectedly:

> He is not human like me: impossible for me to answer
> him
> or appear alongside him in court.
> There is no arbiter between us,
> to lay his hand on both [9:32–33].

Yet the presence of an arbiter will perhaps induce God "to stay his rod from me, or keep away his daunting terrors. Then, even though I cannot win out against him, I shall speak without fear" (9:34–35).[4] To speak without fear is precisely what Job wants. Is there any other way of addressing God for those who really believe in God, provided that God is not mediatized by doctrines that distance, rather than bring God close to them? Thus, at the end of a speech that contains some of the most combative statements of his demand, Job calls for an arbiter who will enable him to speak with God. It becomes increasingly clear as the debate progresses that this arbiter can only be God. Sharp protest and uncertain confidence characterize this first stage in Job's spiritual struggle.

The thought of bringing suit against God—Job sees no alternative at this point—becomes more absorbing. Job moderates his tone in other speeches, but he continues to harp on a deep desire that becomes almost an obsession: to meet and debate with God. Weary of fighting with his friends, he tells them: "My words are intended for Shaddai; I mean to remonstrate with God" (13:3). It is to God that he addresses his lament filled with deep pain but also with lively hope.[5]

Job says that when he appears before God "I shall let my embittered soul speak out" (10:1):

> I shall say to God, "Do not condemn me,
> tell me what your case is against me.
> Is it right for you to attack me,
> in contempt for what you yourself have made,
> thus abetting the schemes of the wicked?
> Are your eyes mere human eyes,
> do you see as human beings see?

Are you mortal like human beings?
  do your years pass as human days pass?
You, who enquire into my faults
  and investigate my sins,
you know very well that I am innocent,
  and that no one can rescue me fron your grasp"
                              [10:2–7].

Job is sure that God knows him to be innocent. His friends do not know it, but God does ("you know very well that I am innocent"). The conviction shows the lofty idea Job has of God; that is why he addresses God boldly but also with the clear conscience of someone who knows to whom he is speaking—namely, to one who is not mortal and whose years do not pass like those of human beings. We, the readers of the Book of Job, also know that he is innocent and that this is how God sees him, for the author of the book has told us so in the prologue. For Job himself, however, the conviction that God knows his true situation is a conviction born of faith.

A WITNESS TO THE DISCUSSION

The theme of the arbiter is developed more fully and the arbiter's identity becomes increasingly clear as Job persists in his case against God and piles up reasons and wishes in connection with it. In face of his friend's stubborn defense of his innocence, Zophar of Naamath reacts with indignation:

These were your words, "My conduct is pure,
  in your eyes I am free of blame!"
Will no one let God speak,
  open his lips and give you answer,
show you the secrets of wisdom
  which put all cleverness to shame?
Then you would realize that God is calling you to
  account for your sin [11:4–6].

"Will no one let God speak?" In Zophar's mouth the words are a threat, but for Job they have become his hope. In the beginning he had said that it would have been better for him not to have been born, but the ongoing debate with his friends has caused him to examine his situation more carefully and to desire to explain it to God. He does not see his way clearly, but he is increasingly persuaded of his innocence and wants to live on in order to make it known—to his friends, and to God, if need be.

Job also realizes, however, that his aspiration to have God appear and debate with God is not a simple matter and may even be dangerous. But he is determined: "I am putting my flesh between my teeth, I am taking my life in my hands; let him kill me if he will; I have no other hope than to justify my conduct in his eyes. And that is what will save me, for the wicked would not dare to appear before him" (13:14–16). Nonetheless, he is afraid of God's power and therefore thinks it prudent to ask for certain guarantees before debating with God:

> Only grant me two concessions,
>   and then I shall not hide away from your face;
> remove your hand, which lies so heavy on me,
>   no longer make me cower from your terror.
> Then call me forward and I shall answer,
>   or rather, I shall speak and you will answer.
> How many faults and crimes have I committed?
>   Tell me what my misdeed has been, what my sin?
>   [13:20–23].

The ways to the dialogue can vary; the important thing is that the Lord should not destroy him but allow him to speak. With the confidence and tender protestation of a child who is frightened by his father's irritation, he says to God:

> Why do you hide your face
>   and look on me as your enemy?
> Do you want to intimidate a wind-blown leaf,
>   do you want to pursue a dry straw? [13:24–25].

Later on, in reply to Eliphaz and after some harsh words to his friends, these "sorry comforters," Job gives free rein to his grief. Dejected and tormented, he complains of God:

> His anger tears and hounds me
>   with gnashing teeth.
> My enemies look daggers at me,
>   and open gaping jaws.
> Their sneers strike like slaps in the face;
>   and they all set on me at once.
> Yes, God has handed me over to the godless,
>   and cast me into the hands of the wicked.
> I was living at peace, until he made me totter,
>   taking me by the neck to shatter me.
> He has set me up as his target:
>   he shoots his arrows at me from all sides,
> pitilessly pierces my loins,
>   and pours my gall out on the ground.

> Breach after breach he drives through me,
>   charging on me like a warrior.
> I have sewn sackcloth over my skin,
>   thrown my forehead in the dust.
> My face is red with tears,
>   and shadow dark as death covers my eyelids.
> Nonetheless, my hands are free of violence,
>   and my prayer is pure [16:9–17].

His is a radical suffering that wounds him in spirit no less than in flesh. But with whatever vitality is left to him, he maintains his innocence unwaveringly ("I was living at peace"; "my hands are free of violence, and my prayer is pure"). Why, then, has God done this to him? Despite everything—his bewilderment and the opposition of the friends who accuse him of blasphemy; his poverty and wretchedness; his feeling of being persecuted and wounded by "the hand of God"—Job glimpses the presence of a witness and a defender. This point is important for him because it fits in with his view that his dispute with God is a kind of lawsuit. In a fine rebuke to the earth, source of the life that is slipping away from him, he expresses a reason for hope:

> Cover not my blood, O earth,
>   and let my cry mount without cease!
> Henceforth I have a witness in heaven,
>   my defender is there on high,
> though my friends mock me
>   and I must weep before God.
> Let him judge between a man and God,
>   between a man and his friend.[6]
> For the years of my life are numbered,
>   and I am leaving by the road of no return [16:18–22].

Convinced though he is of his innocence, Job "fears that his cause may be forever forgotten, and therefore he cries out."[7] He wants his blood not to be buried, in order that it may continue to demand justice for him (see Gen. 4:10; Isa. 26:21; Ezek. 24:7ff.). He will not agree to his case being closed. This dramatic cry, like the complaint in the preceding verses, gives rise nonetheless to an expression of confidence in a mysterious mediator, someone who will defend him in the suit he is carrying on with God (whom, be it noted, he calls his "friend"). He does not say who this person is, but because he knows himself to be innocent, he assumes that there will be someone to bear witness to his uprightness. He assumes, too, that this testimony will be given soon, because his years are numbered and when he is gone there is the danger that justice will not be done him. For the time being he endures sickness and abandonment, puts up with the mockery of his friends' theological arguments, and weeps before God. This is the second phase in Job's spiritual struggle.

MY *GŌ'ĒL* LIVES

During the debate and the maturation that is taking place in Job, there are moments of uncertainty and almost of despair. He says sadly:

> Where then is my hope?
> Who can see any happiness for me?
> Unless they come down to Sheol with me,
> all of us sinking into the dust together [17:15–16].

But this is far from being his final word on the subject. The passages I cited from chapters 9 and 16 were preparing the way for another that shows greater forcefulness and determination, and helps us understand what Job has in mind. But, once again, the act of confidence is preceded by a bitter expression of pain and protest. The latter begins (as in 16:2–5) with a new refusal to accept the arguments of his friends:

> How much longer are you going to torment me
> and crush me by your speeches?
> You have insulted me ten times already:
> have you no shame at maltreating me?
> Even if I had gone astray,
> my error would still be my own affair [19:2–4].

Once again, however, his greater complaint is against God; to God he attributes all his trouble and confusion.[8] He feels harassed by the God in whom he believes:

> I tell you that God has wronged me
> and enveloped me in his net.
> If I protest against such violence, I am not heard;
> if I appeal against it, judgement is never given.
> He has built an impassable wall across my path
> and covered my way with darkness.
> He has deprived me of my glory
> and taken the crown from my head.
> He assails me from all directions to make me vanish;
> he uproots my hope as he might a tree.
> Inflamed with anger against me,
> he regards me as his foe.
> His troops have come in force,
> directing their line of advance towards me,
> they are now encamped around my tent. . . .
> My flesh is rotting under my skin,
> my bones are sticking out like teeth [19:6–12, 20].

All this causes him to ask for mercy on his suffering and for an end to persecution by God and his friends:

> Pity me, pity me, my friends,
>   since I have been struck by the hand of God.
> Must you persecute me just as God does,
>   and give my body no peace? [19:21–22].

Yet Job does not cease to hope in God, although this very confidence is one more element in the heartbreak he is experiencing. Here, as in chapters 9 and 16, in a paroxysm of suffering and demand for justice, he appeals for an arbiter, a mediator, and trusts that he will really find one. This time, however, he delves more deeply into the identity of the person in whom he places his hope.

In this passage, Job makes an act of faith that seems to lack any human basis, and proclaims his deepest conviction:

> I know that I have a living Avenger (*Gō'ēl*)
>   and that at the end he will rise up above the dust.
> After they pull my flesh from me,
>   and I am without my flesh, I shall see God;
> I myself shall see him, and not as a stranger,
>   my own eyes will see him.
> My heart is bursting within my breast [19:25–27].[9]

This is a famous and much-studied passage that has come down to us in a form that makes the reading difficult and therefore susceptible of substantially different translations.[10] In the beginning, after issuing a rhetorical denial that any arbiter was possible in his suit against God, Job had nonetheless called for the presence of such an arbiter (9:33–35). He then, as it were, sketched the silhouette of a mediator (16:18–22, cited above). In the passage now before us he calls this person his *gō'ēl,* his defender or avenger. The word *gō'ēl* came out of the Jewish people's experience of solidarity and had the family for its initial setting; subsequently it found a place in the sphere of the covenant and became a term that emphasized a particular aspect of God's justice. The presence of the theme in the Book of Job is one more example of the link between this work and the traditional faith of Israel.

The verb *ga'al* means to liberate, ransom, redeem. It signifies concretely the obligation the nearest relative has of helping a family member who is in danger of losing his possessions or his freedom or his life.[11] This rescuer is called a *gō'ēl,* an "avenger of blood" (2 Sam. 14:11). The application of the name to Yahweh implies that as a result of the covenant God has become part of the family of the people. God is thus the nearest relative, the one who takes responsibility for the people, the one who rescues them and avenges them if necessary. This notion of God is to be seen especially in Second Isaiah.[12] The word *gō'ēl* thus acquires a religious meaning: God is the defender of all those who suffer injustice. For this reason, Proverbs says:

> Do not remove an ancient landmark
>> or enter the fields of the fatherless;
> for their Redeemer is strong;
>> he will plead their cause against you [23:10–11].

To whom is Job appealing? The subject is much debated, and rightly so, for the passage is one of the high points of the book and crucial for its interpretation. Is Job referring to God or to some third person? In my view, he is referring to God and not to an intermediary distinct from God. Job's cry expresses an anguished but sure hope that comes to him from a profound insight—namely, that God is not to be pigeonholed in the theological categories of his friends. It might almost be said that Job, as it were, splits God in two and produces a God who is judge and a God who will defend him at that supreme moment; a God whom he experiences as almost an enemy but whom he knows at the same time to be truly a friend.[13] He has just now accused God of persecuting him, but at the same time he knows that God is just and does not want human beings to suffer. These are two sides of the one God. This painful, dialectical approach to God is one of the most profound messages of the Book of Job.

At an earlier point, but in a less trenchant way, Job had already appealed to God against God:

> If only you would keep me safe in the abyss
>> and shelter me there till your anger is past,
> and you appoint a place for reconciliation with me!
>>>> [14:13].[14]

God could protect Job against God and God's anger by hiding him in Sheol, which is a kind of nonworld within the world.

A similar splitting of God is seen in a passage of an author who had a keen awareness of human suffering and is representative in so many ways of the suffering peoples of Latin America. That is one reason we have already met him in these pages; I am referring to César Vallejo, whose witness has helped me to understand the Book of Job and relate it more fully to my own experience. Shortly before his death, Vallejo dictated these dramatic and trust-filled lines to his wife Georgette: "Whatever be the cause I must defend before God after death, I myself have a defender: God."[15] In the language of the Bible, he had a *gō'ēl*. This was a God whose fleeting presence he had felt at certain moments in his life; a God who had slipped by him clad in the rags of a lottery-ticket seller and whom he therefore once described as a "bohemian God."[16] At this final moment, in a decisive hour of his life, he sees this God at his side as he faces the judgment that his life has merited from the same God.

The seeming lack of logic in this way of looking at God is simply a sign that any approach to the mystery of God must be complex.[17] Job acknowledges that God passes judgment on human behavior, but he also detects that God's mercy is greater than God's justice or, more accurately, that God's justice is to be understood only in the context of prior and gratuitous love. "I have a living *gō'ēl,*" who will act in behalf of those he loves. Job is sure of this despite appearances[18] and despite the theological artillery of his friends. The experience of near death has brought him to a clear vision of God as the source of life. The God who ("at the end") will not allow him to be destroyed in the world of injustice and loneliness is a living God. God's will that human beings should live is stronger than anything else and represents God's final word.

Job's hope will be confirmed by the vision of God: "I myself shall see him."[19] Not as an enemy or even a stranger[20] but as a friend, someone close to him. Job reaffirms his conviction that he will see God with "his own eyes." This hope causes his heart (literally, his kidney) to burst—that is, it makes him happy in the midst of his trials.

Job is aware of the difficult stretch ahead of him. But his confidence grows that his petition will be heard and that he will be given a meeting with God. He is increasingly sure, moreover, that the outcome will be favorable to him. Therefore he says almost with enthusiasm:

> I should set out my case to him,
>   advancing any number of grievances.
> Then I could learn his defence, every word of it,
>   taking note of everything he said to me.
> Would he put all his strength into this debate with me?
>   No, he would have only to give his attention to me,
> to recognize his opponent as upright
>   and so I should win my case for ever [23:4–7].

Job sees himself already victorious in his struggle with God because he is confident of the reception that he will receive. Perhaps he will go away limping, like Jacob after his contest with God, but—again like Jacob—he believes that he will be declared the winner if he grapples with God in order to receive God's blessing and that he will therefore be able to say in the end: "I have seen God face to face, and yet my life is preserved" (Gen. 32:30).

We have witnessed a gradual increase in Job's faith and hope. From a nebulous request for the presence of an *arbiter* he has advanced to the need of a *witness* and thence finally to an expression of confidence in a *liberator* who will come to rescue him. Each affirmation of hope is immediately preceded by a renewed expression of angry complaint and protest. The spiritual struggle with himself, with his friends, and, above all, with God brings him to a conviction that for the time being amounts to no more than a cry of hope: that he will see, and with his own eyes, his liberator, his *gō'ēl,* and be able to look upon him as a friend.

CHAPTER 9

The Mysterious Meeting
of Two Freedoms

J ob's hope is not in vain: his desire to see God and speak to God is fulfilled. Its fulfillment comes in unexpected ways, but it enables him to make notable progress on the way that leads to correct talk about God. This must take as its starting point a recognition of God's plan and of the fact that because of it the entire work of creation bears the trademark of gratuitousness. It is under that aspect that Yahweh is revealed to Job. Yahweh does not crush Job with divine power but speaks to him of Yahweh's creative freedom and tells him of the respect Yahweh has for human freedom. Job's call for justice is legitimate, and Yahweh is committed to justice. But if justice is to be understood in its full meaning and scope, it must be set in the context of God's overall plan for human history, for it is there that God grants self-revelation. God now waits for an answer from Job, of whose integrity God has been so proud.

AT THE TURNING POINT OF THE WORLD

The response given by the faith of the people was a first approach to an answer. The spiritual struggle Job has undergone has confirmed what is best in that response, and it has enabled him to be critical of the easy, unquestioning acceptance the popular outlook may adopt. Job's confrontation with God, which is presented to us in the Book of Job with a boldness unmatched elsewhere in the Bible, contributes to our fund of mystical language about God. The confrontation will end in a full acknowledgment of the greatness and freedom of God. Spiritual struggle thus proves to be a means by which Job comes to understand more fully and deeply the language of popular faith (Job, chaps. 1 and 2) with its riches and ambiguities, and is helped to move on to contemplation of the mystery of God (see chap. 42).

Job's last plea ended with a shout of challenge and a dramatic call for an answer:

> Will no one give me a hearing?
> This is my signature![1] Now let Shaddai reply!
> When my adversary has drafted his writ against me
> I shall wear it on my shoulder,
> and bind it round my head like a royal turban.
> I shall give him an account of my every step
> and go as boldly as a prince to meet him [31:35–37].

Job persists in regarding the Almighty as an adversary. He wants the case to be set forth clearly; therefore he expects the arguments against him to be written down so that everyone can read them. Job also betrays a feeling of anticipated victory ("I shall . . . go as boldly as a prince to meet him"). Above all, he issues a clear challenge: let God speak, the God who has plunged him into poverty and suffering. When Job is done speaking, the narrator says laconically: "End of the words of Job" (31:40). And his statement is correct: Job will not speak again except to say that henceforth he will acknowledge the gratuitousness of God's love and will know how to enter fully into it.

God then speaks (after the interlude of Elihu's speeches, which we have already seen). There is no one else there but Job. He will not again listen to the satan, the three friends, and Elihu; their scolding and clever remarks have faded away. Only Job and his God remain. Here is the encounter Job has so feared but also so awaited. In the person of Job, alone here before God, are present all the innocent of this world who suffer unjustly and ask "why?" of the God in whom they believe.

God speaks, but in an unpredictable way—making no reference to concrete problems and therefore not responding to the distress and questions of Job.[2] This does not seem correct. What God says is disconcerting to the reader, but Job seems to understand it (see 40:3–4, and 42:1–6). Our aim is to share this understanding.

God answers Job—because it is indeed a matter of God's responding to Job's insistent plea—"from the heart of the tempest." This is a classic image used in the Bible to highlight an important self-manifestation of God. The phrase is used twice here (38:1; 40:6), following the same pattern as at other key points in the Book of Job. Furthermore, on both occasions—that is, at the beginning of God's two speeches—the author calls God "Yahweh"; this is the classical name of the God of the covenant and has not been used since the prologue.

Job has fearfully anticipated the way in which God would speak to him: "He will crush me in the tempest and wound me over and over without cause" (9:17).[3] This fear of God's self-manifestation is a common theme in the Bible (see Exod. 20:18–20). But the fear proves mistaken. God does not crush the addressee, but returns to the theme of God's own greatness. Job had referred to this several times (adding complaints, it is true), and Elihu had made it the focus of the second part of his speech. On the lips of God, however, the subject takes on a special emphasis and has a different purpose. The greatness of God is to be identified less with power than with freedom and gratuitous love—and with tenderness.

Job has succeeded in getting God to answer him. He has demanded this response stubbornly and in different ways. God speaks to him; God does not crush him or rebuke him for his sins. Job had boldly challenged God: "How many faults and crimes have I committed? Tell me what my misdeed has been, what my sin?" (13:23). God does not do so; God's answer follows a different tactic. Job's friends are now proven wrong: in their eyes he was guilty and therefore responsible for the evils that had befallen him, but God says nothing of any guilt and thus confirms his innocence.

I must emphasize the point, moreover, that although it is important that God agrees to answer Job, this by itself is not enough. Some interpreters of the Book of Job are so disconcerted by the fact of God's speaking that they pay too little attention to the content of the speeches; they think what God says is less significant than the fact of the speaking, the presence, of God. In their view, the very presence of God satisfies the deepest desires of Job who has been asking and even demanding this presence.[4] I do not think that this is a correct view, for the content of God's speeches specify and concretize the response; the words of God give the presence of God its full meaning.[5]

Yahweh speaks twice (chaps. 38–39 and 40:7–41).[6] Each speech has its proper theme: the first emphasizes the *plan* of God, which enfolds and gives meaning to God's creative work; the second emphasizes God's *just government* of the world. The literary beauty of these chapters (the author reserves his best writing for the speeches of Job and God) only underscores the power of the message. At the same time, the poetic language gives the text a forward movement that links topic to topic, and invites the reader to enter more and more deeply into the meaning.

The tone of challenge now comes from Yahweh: "Who is this, obscuring my intentions with his ignorant words?" (38:2). "Intentions" or "plans" translates the Hebrew *'ēṣāh* (see Isa. 14:26; 19:17; 25:1; 28:29; Jer. 32:19–20; Prov. 19:21), which means a plan of action, a project. After studying a good number of passages, Lévêque comes to the conclusion that "one constant is inescapable: the *'ēṣāh* of God always refers to God's action *in history*, whether of the nations or of Israel or of individuals."[7] This is true of Job 38:2. In his speeches Job has really been questioning the intentions or plans of God. More specifically, in his suffering and in his rejection of the explanation given of it by his friends, he has expressed doubts about God's justice (not about the government of the material world). He has thus been "obscuring my intentions," and Yahweh will therefore seek to specify and clarify the meaning of the divine will in human history. This is what God does; the interpretation of God's words depends on keeping this purpose in mind. God's plan has its origin in the gratuitousness of creative love.

The confrontational attitude continues, but now it is found on the side of God who tells Job to ready himself for the fight: "Brace yourself like a fighter; I am going to ask the questions, and you are to inform me" (38:3). "Brace yourself"—literally, "gird your loins"—was a Hebrew expression signifying to ready oneself for a difficult task, for a struggle. From the outset Yahweh attacks Job's presupposition and prepares the way for the main burden of the message. God asks ironically:

> Where were you when I laid the earth's foundation?
>> Tell me, since you are so well-informed!
> Who decided its dimensions, do you know?
>> Or who stretched the measuring line across it?
> What supports its pillars at their bases?
>> Who laid its cornerstone
> to the joyful concert of the morning stars
>> and unanimous acclaim of the sons of God?
> Who pent up the sea behind closed doors
>> when it leaped tumultuous from the womb,
> when I wrapped it in a robe of mist
>> and made black clouds its swaddling bands;
> when I cut out the place I had decreed for it
>> and imposed gates and a bolt?
> "Come so far," I said, "and no further;
>> here your proud waves must break" [38:4–11].

Yahweh goes directly to the source of all existing things, to the place and time when everything began. "The earth's foundation," "its pillars at their bases," "cornerstone"—all are expressive images. The friends and Job himself thought that the world had been made in order to be immediately useful to human beings and to be of service in temporal retribution: a reward for the just, a punishment for sinners. This they regarded as the reason for God's work, and therefore in their view God's action in history must take foreseeable paths. But God attacks Job energetically on precisely this point: Where were you when I set up the pillars of creation? If Job is "so well informed" ("if you know understanding" [Hebrew, *bīnāh*] would be a literal translation of v. 4)— that is, if he is capable of discernment—let him answer.

Job in fact came later on the scene, after God had contained the sea behind bolted doors; he is therefore disqualified to say anything about the foundation of the world. God who has been able to restrain the pride of the sea now does the same for the excessive pretensions of Job and his friends, who try to establish limits and pathways for God's action in history.

At the very beginning of the speech, Yahweh expresses willingness to reveal the plan or intention, the *'ēṣāh*, of God. This revelation requires *bīnāh* on Job's part—that is, understanding, discernment, knowledge of the truth of things.[8] The revelation of God's plan, when received with good judgment, will show Job that the doctrine of retribution is not the key to understanding the universe; this doctrine can give rise only to a commonplace relationship of self-interest with God and others. The reason for believing "for nothing"—the theme set at the beginning of the book—is the free and gratuitous initiative taken by divine love. This is not something connected only indirectly with the work of creation or something added on to it; it is the very hinge on which the world turns. This is the only motive for creation that can lead to a communion of two freedoms. It must therefore be the point from which we always start in order to make all things new. The opening verses thus show the line that will be followed in Yahweh's speeches.

Next comes a series of questions in which the theme of the wicked appears, and the question of divine justice and human freedom is hinted at:

> Have you ever in your life given orders to the morning
> > or sent the dawn to its post,
> to grasp the earth by its edges
> > and shake the wicked out of it?
> She turns it red as a clay seal,
> > she tints it as though it were a dress,
> stealing the light from evil-doers
> > and breaking the arm raised to strike [38:12–15].

Morning is the time of God's action (see Ps. 90:14; 5:3). It is the time for just action—unlike the night, which favors evildoers—but it does not get rid of the wicked; its light continues to shine on them. Is creation therefore botched? I shall come back to this passage, which puts forward in an unobtrusive way the central theme of the second speech. For the moment, God continues to overwhelm Job with questions which he cannot answer but which build up a sense of beauty and gratuitousness:

> Have you been right down to the sources of the sea
> > and walked about at the bottom of the Abyss?
> Have you been shown the gates of Death,
> > have you seen the janitors of the Shadow dark as
> > > death?
> Have you an inkling of the extent of the earth?
> > Tell me all about it if you have!
> Which is the way to the home of the Light,
> > and where does darkness live?—
> You could then show them the way to their proper
> > places,
> > you could put them on the path home again!
> > > > > > > > [38:16–20].

After this broadside of questions, God pretends that Job knows the answers, and says sarcastically: "You must know, because you were born then and are very old now" (38:21).[9] The verses that follow are marked by the pleasure and joy God takes in the work of creation, and they bring out the message of the speeches: the gratuitousness of God's doings. This it is that gives meaning to God's "justice":

> Who bores a channel for the downpour
>   or clears the way for the rolling thunder
> so that rain may fall on lands where no one lives,
>   and the deserts void of human dwelling,
> to meet the needs of the lonely wastes
>   and make grass sprout on the thirsty ground?
>
> [38:25–27].

In the Bible rain is often looked upon as a means of rewarding human behavior and of punishing it as well: although it gives life, it can also destroy. There is no reference here to rain as an instrument of divine justice; it is mentioned rather in connection with "lands where no one lives" and "deserts void of human dwelling." What purpose does rain have in such places? It contributes nothing but is lost fruitlessly in the wilderness, in places empty of human history. Can Job and his friends comprehend this? Or do we perhaps find ourselves in a world of the arbitrary, the strange, the self-willed?[10]

The questions continue. The irony that also continues is an important characteristic of God's speeches; it is doubtless one of the achievements intended by the author of the Book of Job. It enables him to treat in a subtle way a theme that is both rich and full of tensions. The main idea has now been established: in the beginning was the gratuitousness of divine love; it—not retribution—is the hinge on which the world turns. It is significant that the poet places this emphatic affirmation of gratuitousness in the mouth of Yahweh, God of the covenant, who is just and requires justice.

THE FREEDOM OF GOD

God assails the pretended knowledge of Job and even more than that of his friends, who regard everything as foreseen and think they know for certain when and how God has punished sinners. What God is criticizing here is every theology that presumes to pigeonhole the divine action in history and gives the illusory impression of knowing it in advance. The outlook God is rejecting is obviously the one that Job's theologian friends defend and, despite himself, Job shares at bottom. God will bring him to see that nothing, not even the world of justice, can shackle God; this is the very heart of the answer. Let us examine it.

The justice of God has been the main subject of the debate. For Eliphaz and his companions, whose theology focuses on principles, the doctrine of retribution expresses God's justice. In keeping with it, God gives to individuals according to their deserts. When seen in this perspective, Job's sufferings are the result of his guilt. There is no room for doubt on this point, for the ethical order is crystal clear. The only recourse for Job, then, is to repent and ask forgiveness of his sins. God, who is merciful, will receive him back; this too is part of the order God has established.

Job for his part starts with his own experience. He knows that he is indeed a sinner like every other human being, but he declares himself innocent as far as his sufferings are concerned. In the eyes of his three friends and, with certain reservations, in the eyes of Job himself, such a claim implies guilt on God's part. According to the theologian friends, this is blasphemy. For Job it is a blind alley, and this is why he wants to debate the matter directly with God.[11]

The theme of justice and gratuitousness is subtly present in God's speeches; I have cited two of the most important passages to illustrate this (see 38:12–15 and 25–27). But it must be remembered (this is one of the reasons why the speeches disconcert some) that chapters 38–41 deal seemingly with the world of nature, not the world of history. Nonetheless we must not forget that the first speech began with a reference to the plan ('ēṣāh) of God in history. The references to justice will therefore have to be seen as part of the great cosmic fresco that the speeches create.

The speeches say that God indeed has a plan, but it is not one that the human mind can grasp so as to make calculations based on it and foresee the divine action. God is free; God's love is a cause, not an effect that is, as it were, handcuffed.[12] After God has spoken of the inanimate world, symbolic reference is made to divine freedom in the fine verses on the various animals that elude human control and whose "calves, having grown big and strong, go off into the desert and never come back to them" (39:4):

> Who has given the wild donkey his freedom,
>   who has undone the harness of the brayer?
> I have given him the wastelands as his home,
>   the salt plain as his habitat.
> He scorns the turmoil of the town,
>   obeys no donkey-man's shouts.
> The mountains are the pastures that he ranges
>   in quest of anything green.
> Is the wild ox willing to serve you
>   or spend a night beside your manger?
> If you tie a rope around his neck
>   will he harrow the furrows for you?
> Can you rely on his massive strength
>   and leave him to do your heavy work?
> Can you depend on him to come home
>   and pile your grain on your threshing-floor?
>   [39:5–12].

Here is the freedom of the donkey who roams wild in the wastelands, the refusal of the wild ox to submit to domestic tasks (later there will be references to the hawk and the eagle who "make their eyrie in the heights"; see 39:26–30).

Is everything that exists in the natural world really meant to be domesticated by human beings and subjected to their service? Furthermore, Job has said that to be free, one must be far from God, in that dead place and place of the dead that is Sheol. There, he said sorrowfully, "the slave is free of his master" (3:19). Now in a new irony Yahweh teaches him that, on the contrary, if the animals described are free, it is because they keep far away from human beings and because God takes delight in them.[13]

God's speeches are a forceful rejection of a purely anthropocentric view of creation. Not everything that exists was made to be directly useful to human beings; therefore, they may not judge everything from their point of view. The world of nature expresses the freedom and delight of God in creating. It refuses to be limited to the narrow confines of the cause-effect relationship.

The text goes on to point out an apparent incongruity in creation—the ostrich, which is slow-witted yet graceful:

> The ostrich flaps its wings proudly,
>   its feathers are like the feathers of the stork.[14]
> She leaves her eggs on the ground
>   with only earth to warm them;
> forgetting that a foot may tread on them
>   or a wild animal crush them.
> Cruel to her chicks as if they were not hers,
>   little she cares if her labour goes for nothing.
> God, you see, has deprived her of wisdom
>   and given her no share of intelligence.
> Yet if she bestirs herself to use her height
>   she can make fools of horse and rider too [39:13–18].

The possibility cannot be excluded that the "bohemian God" (as Vallejo would say) who speaks in these discourses is playing with Job.[15] This is suggested by the insinuation that at times, as in the case of the ostrich, God has forgotten to give animals their share of understanding or wisdom (*bīnāh*) (v. 17). This is an invitation to Job to learn from God's plan and thus show that he is not lacking in discernment. At the same time, however, the God who is sarcastic and amused also reassures him: Job, like the ostrich, may have lacked wisdom in his life, but he is still pleasing to God the creator.

Next comes the finest bit of poetry in this chapter—the verses on the horse:

> Are you the one who makes the horse so brave
>   and covers his neck with a flowing mane?
> Do you make him leap like a grasshopper?
>   His haughty neighing inspires terror.
> Exultantly he paws the soil of the valley,
>   and charges the battle-line in all his strength.
> He laughs at fear; he is afraid of nothing,
>   he recoils before no sword.

On his back the quiver rattles,
    the flashing spear and javelin.
Trembling with impatience, he eats up the miles;
    when the trumpet sounds, there is no holding him.
At each trumpet blast he neighs exultantly.
    He scents the battle from afar,
    the thundering of the commanders and the war cry
[39:19–25].

All these passages on the animals breathe out an air of freedom, vigor, and independence. God is pleased with creation (see Gen. 1:31). The whole of this first speech (chaps. 38–39) expresses the delight that the created world gives God. If the rain falls on the bleak moors, this is not because of any necessity but because it pleases God. Utility is not the primary reason for God's action; the creative breath of God is inspired by beauty and joy. Job is invited to sing with Yahweh the wonders of creation—without forgetting that the source of it all is the free and gratuitous love of God.

The reasoning in God's discourse seems to be this: what holds for the world of nature, holds with all the greater reason for the world of history. There is therefore an implied question: Must all that happens in history, including God's action, necessarily fit hand in glove with the theological categories that reason has developed? The power of the argument is all the more understandable in that for the Bible, with its unified outlook in which nonetheless there is no confusion of levels, creation is seen as a saving action of God.[16]

This means that it is difficult and even impossible to discover in detail the reasons for God's action, so as to be able to foresee it and, as it were, manage it. Job's friends, unlike Job himself, seek not so much to see God as to foresee what God will do. They are determined to lay hands on God instead of abandoning themselves to God's embrace and, in the words of Deuteronomy, "cleaving to" God, thereby choosing life (30:19–20). The speeches of God to Job, on the contrary, are a reminder of "the incomprehensible character of God," which, as Christian Duquoc rightly says, "indicates the freedom and gratuitousness of God."[17]

HUMAN LITTLENESS AND RESPECT FOR GOD

Yahweh ends the first speech with a direct and explicit challenge: "Is Yahweh's opponent going to give way? Has God's critic thought up an answer?" (40:2). Contrary to those who claim that the Lord has said nothing to Job about his problems, the author believes that Yahweh has indeed said something that Job can understand. Perhaps Job will now abandon his protests, and therefore God asks him to speak. In any case, Job now has the right to reply, and the conditions for doing so have been met.

The flood of questions, the irony they reflect, the difficulty of answering them, and the satisfaction produced in him by God's presence—all these cause

Job to lose the self-assurance with which he had sought this meeting. Conquered perhaps, but not convinced, he attempts to retreat a step:

> I feel my littleness: what reply shall I give?[18]
> I had better lay my hand over my mouth.
> I have spoken once, I shall not speak again;
>   I have spoken twice, I have nothing more to say
>   [40:4–5].

This is Job's first answer to the speeches of the Lord, or, better, it is a statement that he will not give an answer, a declaration that he will remain silent. He acknowledges his littleness but does not admit he has sinned; he expresses humility but not resignation. Job feels himself to be little (literally: trivial, of little weight)—that is, unimportant, of little value. His tone is quite different now; earlier he had gone so far as to assert his own importance (19:9; 29:20). The speeches of God have brought home the fact that human beings are not the center of the universe and that not everything has been made for their service. Acknowledgment of his littleness may thus be an important step toward the abandonment of his anthropocentrism.

There is, however, no repentance. Job knows himself to be innocent. He has said so over and over, and he still thinks so; nor does God accuse him.[19] Henceforth he will remain silent and place his hand over his mouth, as his friends would have had to do if they had listened to his arguments (see 21:5); and as did those who in the good times used to marvel at his wisdom (cf. 29:9).

Job now knows more about God, but he does not yet know enough. The light has still not dawned fully for him. His struggle has been too extensive and profound for him to change his opinion easily. The poet shows finesse in getting this resistance across to the reader. Job is still full of his own problems; his answer is given in the first person singular. It will take a costly effort for him to go out of himself and his world. In his proposal to withdraw, any reference to God is only implicit.

Yahweh, however, will not let go. Yahweh refuses to let Job withdraw from the debate; Yahweh has more to say. Moreover, Job must get to the bottom of this matter; he must drink to the full the cup of protest. Motivated perhaps by Job's resistance, Yahweh begins a new speech. This time, as I said earlier, the principal theme is not the plan (*'ēṣāh*) of God with its basis in gratuitousness, but God's just government of the world, God's justice, judgment (*mishpaṭ*). This was the question on which Job had focused more directly. To approach it in a profitable way, however, it was necessary to locate it in the context of God's overall plan. That is what God did in the first speech.[20]

Once more Yahweh answers Job "from the heart of the tempest" and tells him a second time to "gird up his loins": "brace yourself as a fighter." Once again he asks Job to answer questions: "I am going to ask the questions, and you are to inform me!" (40:6–7).[21] God does not want resigned silence that hides murmurs of dissatisfaction. This time, however, the challenge

will be harder and more specific: Job must choose between God and himself:

> Do you really want to reverse my judgement,
>   put me in the wrong and yourself in the right? [40:8].

The theme of justice is undoubtedly the one that electrifies the air around
Job and his God. In light of what we saw in the first two sections of this
chapter, Yahweh's question amounts to saying: Do you persist in staying locked
into a world of easy explanations? Are you going to dispute my right to control
what comes upon you? Are you trying to imprison my free and gratuitous love
in your theological concepts? Do you want to make yourself judge of my
actions?

In that kind of universe, God would not be God. It must be said, moreover,
that these words are addressed not only to Job but to all those who, like Job's
friends, seek to domesticate God, subject God to their will, decide whom God
is to favor, and thus attempt to win a privileged place for themselves in human
society.

God will help Job—and in him all of us—to escape from his prison by
showing him that he will be in the right only if he occupies the place that is
properly his as a human being and a believer. With profound irony God asks:

> Has your arm the strength of God's,
>   can your voice thunder as loud?
> Come on, display your majesty and grandeur,
>   robe yourself in splendour and glory.
> Let the fury of your anger burst forth,
>   humble the haughty at a glance!
> Bury the lot of them in the ground,
>   shut them, every one, in the Dungeon.
> And I shall be the first to pay you homage,
>   since your own right hand is strong enough to save
>   you [40:9–14].

That the words are ironic is clear. But this time there is no mention of God's
power or of God's delight in creation or of God's sense of humor. Rather the
Lord is explaining, tenderly and, as it were, shyly, that the wicked cannot
simply be destroyed with a glance. God wants justice indeed, and desires that
divine judgment (*mishpaṭ*) reign in the world; but God cannot impose it, for the
nature of created beings must be respected. God's power is limited by human
freedom; for without freedom God's justice would not be present within
history. Furthermore, precisely because human beings are free, they have the
power to change their course and be converted. The destruction of the wicked
would put an end to that possibility.

In other words, the all-powerful God is also a "weak" God. The mystery of divine freedom leads to the mystery of human freedom and to respect for it. The Bible shows God's self-revelation in contrasting situations (see Ps. 139). A theophany can occur in the midst of fire (see Exod. 3:3–5) or when a storm erupts in thunder and flashes of lightning (see Exod. 19:16). But God also dispenses self-revelation shyly and almost imperceptibly, with a gentle caress:

> And [the Lord] said, "Go forth, and stand upon the mount before the Lord." And behold, the Lord passed by, and a great and strong wind rent the mountains, and broke in pieces the rocks before the Lord, but the Lord was not in the wind; and after the wind an earthquake, but the Lord was not in the earthquake; and after the earthquake a fire, but the Lord was not in the fire; and after the fire a still small voice. And when Elijah heard it, he wrapped his face in his mantle and went out and stood at the entrance of the cave. And behold, there came a voice to him, and said, "What are you doing here, Elijah?" [1 Kings 19:11–13].

God is manifest not in the mighty wind or the earthquake or the fire but very tactfully in the whisper of a gentle breeze that is incapable of crushing or burying anyone.

This respect for human freedom was only hinted at in a passage to which I called attention earlier: 38:12–15.[22] It was said there in a beautiful image that the light of dawn "grasps the earth by its edges and shakes the wicked out of it," preventing their misdeeds. But there is also the implication that the wicked are not simply annihilated. In fact, the image of morning succeeding each night conveys the idea of an ongoing task symbolized by the light of day: the task of establishing justice.[23]

On the other hand, there is this extremely important point: just as we cannot speak of the wicked as if they had always been such and must go on being such, neither can we say that the just will never cease to be just. Consequently, the respect God shows here for human freedom is given equally to those who have thus far been devout and moral individuals. It is given therefore to Job no less than to others; God respects him too and will not destroy him immediately if he acts wrongly or wickedly.

Yahweh, the "I am," the protector of life, urges Job to acknowledge the divine mercy, even if he does not fully understand it, and to address it as the author of the Book of Wisdom does:

> But thou art merciful to all, for thou canst do all things,
> and thou dost overlook men's sins, that they may
>   repent.
> For thou lovest all things that exist,
> and hast loathing for none of the things which thou hast
>   made,
> for thou wouldst not have made anything if thou hadst
>   hated it.

> How would anything have endured if thou hadst not
>   willed it?
> Or how would anything not called forth by thee have
>   been preserved?
> Thou sparest all things, for they are thine, O Lord who
>   lovest the living [11:23–26; see Hos. 11:9].

In his first answer to God, Job had spoken of his littleness, his insignificance—that is, the littleness and insignificance of any human being as compared with God and God's creative work. Yahweh accepts this acknowledgment with a corresponding expression of humility: Yahweh too has limits, which are self-imposed. Human beings are insignificant in Job's judgment, but they are great enough for God, the almighty, to stop at the threshold of their freedom and ask for their collaboration in the building of the world and in its just governance.

Is Job able to understand this hard and demanding, but also friendly and respectful, message? Later on, in his final answer, he will speak of "marvels that are beyond my grasp" (42:3). The "marvels" refer both to the works the mighty God has done in this world and to those of the "weak" God who is heedful of human freedom and its historical rhythm.

But what this God of grace and justice cannot do, neither will Job succeed in doing. To claim otherwise would be to seek to usurp God's place. We must reflect on the scope of the last verse in the passage cited: "I shall be the first to pay you homage, since your own right hand is strong enough to save you" (40:14). The words used are technical. The word translated "homage" is used of the worship owed to God,[24] and it is a classic theme of the Bible that only the right hand of God is capable of saving.[25] In other words, God is telling Job that if he can do what is impossible to God, God will treat him as God.

The statement has the sarcastic edge that we saw previously. Yet, in simple truth, the logic at work in a knowledge that claims to know everything about the Lord, to account fully for the Lord's actions, and to foresee how the Lord will intervene, leads in the final analysis to the replacement of God with self and to the usurpation of God's place. It leads, in other words, to the denial of God. The god who subsequently asserts itself will be in the final analysis a prefabricated, domesticated god made by human hands (see Isa. 44:14–17). This is precisely what the Bible means by idolatry, which is a permanent temptation for believers, as many passages of the Bible warn us. The irony God employs in this passage is therefore simply a means of bringing home to Job the end result of a certain kind of rational pride—the replacement of God by the human person.[26]

The reference is undoubtedly to the theology of Job's friends. But as I have several times pointed out, Job himself to some extent accepts the same outlook; he has never succeeded in ridding himself of it completely despite his sometimes savage attempts to criticize it.

Yahweh reinforces what has just been said in this key passage by bringing two fanciful animals on the scene: Behemoth and Leviathan.[27] The passage is a difficult one, and many interpretations are given of the meaning of the two fabulous beasts.[28] The most plausible approach, in my view, is to regard them as a kind of illustration of the opening verses of God's second speech and, concretely, as symbols of the wicked. Yahweh is using these animals to remind us that, like everything that exists, the enormous forces of chaos and disorder are subject to divine power, even if it does not annihilate them.

From the opening words the emphasis is on the creatureliness of these mighty beasts: "Look at Behemoth, my creature, just as you are!" (40:15). Job has a trait in common with these animals: all have come from God's hand. They are, as it were, holdovers from the chaos out of which the world, the cosmos, emerged. Because of his undeserved suffering, Job sees existence as a chaos, a continuation of the original disorder. God is trying to show Job that divine power controls these chaotic forces, although at the same time God says that they will not be destroyed. They represent the wicked of whom God has just been speaking (40:11–13); they are forces existing in the world. The Lord does not forthwith put an end to these remnants of the original chaos (into which Job has felt himself being thrust), but the Lord does control them. There is evil in the world, but the world is not evil. There are chaotic forces within the cosmos, but the cosmos is not a chaos.[29]

The text of 40:7–14 and the ensuing illustration of it are thus an important part of God's argument.[30] The still rather unconvinced Job of the first reply is brought face to face here with the subject that has been preoccupying him: justice. God's *first speech* was focused on the revelation of the divine plan (*'ēṣāh*, 38:2); gratuitousness is the hinge on which the world turns and the definitive seal set upon it. This is the reality that embraces and gives meaning to everything. Only in its light is it possible to understand correctly the scope and meaning of the subject taken up in the *second speech*: God's will that divine justice and judgment (*mishpaṭ*, 40:7) be established.[31]

The correlate of the divine freedom God has revealed to Job is human freedom. The first calls to and establishes the second. The final chapters of the Book of Job tell us of the meeting of these two freedoms. Job's freedom finds expression in his complaints and rebellion; God's freedom finds expression in the gratuitousness of the divine love that refuses to be confined within a system of predictable rewards and punishments. Job's freedom reaches its full maturity when he encounters without intermediaries the God in whom he hopes; God's freedom comes to light in the revelation that divine gratuitous love has been made the foundation of the world and that only in light of this fact can the meaning of divine justice be grasped. When human freedom meets the divine freedom it also penetrates to the depths of itself.

God's speeches are thus concerned directly in a very coherent way with the subject that has been discussed throughout the entire book. There could be no more radical rejection of the theologian friends who have not known how to speak correctly of God. Then come God's final words:

Who can stand up to me?
Who will resist me and go away unscathed?
Everything under heaven is mine [41:2–3].[32]

These verses recall the last defiant words of Job in chapter 31: "Here is my signature!" (v. 35). The Lord's signature follows: "Everything under heaven is mine." Everything that is and happens bears in some way God's trademark; that is why human beings do not understand it completely.

Now Job speaks once again.

CHAPTER 10

My Eyes Have Seen You

J ob makes his second and final reply to God. It is very different in tone from his first answer, for as the result of a long and painful process he has ceased to resist. No longer does he express simply an honest but still vague acceptance of his littleness. This time there is something deeper, because what he has heard and seen has caused him to abandon his grumbling and return—but on a new basis—to his initial reaction of reverence for God (see the prologue). A study of Job's second reply will enable us to see what the true relationship is between *justice* and *gratuitousness;* this, in my opinion, is the key to the interpretation of the Book of Job.

SURRENDER TO LOVE

Job's first reply to God was focused on himself; that is why he spoke in the first person singular. Here, on the contrary, the point of reference is God: God's plans, God's words, God's presence. Job's attitude has changed, therefore, though there is still no acknowledgment of any sins that supposedly have brought deserved suffering upon him. His conviction of innocence is deep-seated. But, as I pointed out earlier, at no time does God accept the accusations made by Job's theologian friends. God thus implicitly confirms the integrity of Job, whose own unyielding and heartrending assertion of it has called in question an entire way of understanding God and the relationship of human beings to God.

The beautiful passage that I am going to study here does show, however, that there has been a transformation in Job. The change is due to his understanding of God's speeches, for these—despite interpretations to the contrary—have given an answer to his profound anxieties.[1] It is not indeed the kind of answer he had been looking for, and yet it brings the fulfillment of his hopes. The Lord's words have released him from the cell in which he had found himself imprisoned because of the contradiction between his experience of his own innocence and the doctrine of retribution. He had had the courage to face up to the contradiction and to proclaim it for all to hear.

From the depths of the abyss and even in the cruelest suffering ("Vermin and loathsome scabs cover my body; my skin is cracked and oozes pus"—7:5), he had asserted his right to speak:

> That is why I will not restrain my tongue:[2]
>   in my anguish of spirit I shall speak,
>   in my bitterness of soul I shall complain [7:11].

It was a difficult and even tortuous road he had to travel in order to speak of God. But was it the only road? Or perhaps the best? We must examine in some detail the following very important passage:

1. This was the answer Job gave to Yahweh:
2. I know that you are all-powerful and there is no plan you cannot carry out.
3. (You said:) "Who is this that blurs my plans with ignorant words?"
    —It is true: I spoke without understanding
      marvels that are beyond my grasp.
4. (You said:) "Listen to me, for I am going to speak;
    I am going to ask the questions, and you are to inform me."
5. I once knew you only by hearsay,
    now my eyes have seen you;
6. therefore I repudiate and repent
    of dust and ashes [42:1-6].[3]

There are three steps in this response of Job: an acknowledgment that God has plans and that these are being carried out; a discovery of previously unrecognized aspects of reality; a joyous encounter with the Lord. All this has an inevitable consequence: the abandonment of his attitude of complaint and sadness. The first step (v. 2) is a reaffirmation of something he had already maintained earlier; the second (v. 3) and third (vv. 4-5) give expression to discoveries made in the light of God's speeches. The explicit references to the beginning of both of God's speeches (38:2-3; 40:7) make it clear that Job's answer has to do with what God has been saying to him.

1. Yahweh has asked Job over and over what he, Job, knows and understands (Hebrew, *yd'*) about the divine works. Here Job uses the same verb "know" to express what he has just learned and now has as his deepest conviction. "I know" was also the phrase he used when he spoke of his conviction that his *gō'ēl*, the God who liberates, would defend him (see 19:25). Job thus begins here with a profession of faith in the power of God. He had expressed substantially the same faith earlier in arguing with his friends; here, however, there are nuances that need to be brought out.

Right at the beginning, God reproached Job for trying to obscure the divine plans (see 38:2). God asserted that such plans do indeed exist, but they do not, as it were, possess or control God; much less, then, is God controlled by those human beings who claim to know God's intentions in detail. Rather the contrary is true, for, as God said in the second speech, "everything under heaven is mine" (41:3). Job now knows that "there is no plan you cannot carry out,"[4] even if the human mind cannot always comprehend the manner of its execution. God does indeed have plans, and the world is not a chaos as Job had pictured it in his opening monologue and as he had suggested again later on at the most decisive moments in the dispute with his friends. His reasoning had been, more or less, that "I do not understand these plans; therefore they do not exist." He never stated this in so many words, but it was the logical conclusion of his argument with Eliphaz and his companions.

As a matter of fact, what Job was really rejecting was, first, the moral order as presented to him by his theologian friends and, secondly and consequently, the God to whom they appealed. If there is no alternative to the doctrine of temporal retribution, then for someone who has experienced what Job has experienced, the conclusion is inevitable: the world is indeed a chaos. If the only possible order is the order of justice that his friends proclaim, then Job must become, even against his will, a defender of disorder, because his fate will be the same whether or not he is upright and innocent (9:15–20). The proof that this position into which he has been forced never satisfied him is his ardent plea that he might debate the matter not with his friends but with God. In his lamentation (which is a form of prayer) Job, like Jeremiah, was close to God, closer than were his friends with their theology. Job has at various moments acknowledged the greatness of God (see 9:4, 34–35; 12:19; 13:21–22; 23:4–6); now he knows that one manifestation of divine power is that God has plans and carries them out in an utterly free manner.

2. In his final answer Job next cites (v. 3) what God had said at the beginning of the first speech (38:2). God there spoke of a plan or intention (*'ēṣāh*) in which God's gratuitous love is the ground of all existence. Job's answer is inspired by these speeches of God.[5] What he has now heard from the mouth of Yahweh has given him a glimpse of another world, an order different from the one he rejected but for which until now there seemed to be no alternative. All this is still not entirely clear to him, but at least he is no longer being suffocated by the religious universe of his friends and indeed of his age.

The words of God that Job cites in v. 3 have made him realize his own limits: he had been speaking "without understanding," literally "without intelligence," "without discernment"—that is, without the *bīnāh* for lack of which the Lord has rebuked him. Job's words here are a new and specific reference to God's first speech, in which, as I pointed out, the idea of the discernment whereby Job ought to be attuned to God's plan played a key role. A change has begun, for Job now realizes that there are "marvels that are beyond my grasp."[6] The important thing here, it should be noted, is not Job's admiration for the magnificence of creation[7] but rather his recognition of the plan, the *'ēṣāh,* of God (see Yahweh's first speech). It is a plan of gratuitous love, and it is in light of this love that God's will to justice, God's *mishpaṭ,* in the governance of the world, reveals its full meaning (see the second speech).

The questions Yahweh inexorably pursued have revealed to Job the freedom and love that permeate God's plan. As a result, Job can speak of hitherto unsuspected facets of reality that he does not fully understand but that are not therefore any less real. He is not saying that he has acquired any further information from all that God has said; on the contrary, these wonders too are beyond his ability to grasp completely, but he has indeed begun to understand, to acquire the needed discernment. He still has a long road to travel. Previously, when he moved within the framework of the doctrine of retribution, he did not have any journey at all ahead of him because at bottom everything was (supposedly) understood, and he was already at the goal. This is no longer the case; he sees things differently now. God is present to him as an abiding newness.

3. In a further explicit reference to the first and second speeches Job once again cites God: "Listen to me, for I am going to speak; I am going to ask the questions, and you are to inform me" (v. 4). The salvo of questions launched by God, as well as the direct dialogue at last granted to Job have left him no choice but to acknowledge humbly and joyfully an encounter that has changed his life: "I once knew you only by hearsay, now my eyes have seen you" (42:5). As I noted above, the verb "know" plays an important role in God's speeches, which are a lengthy and penetrating challenge to Job's knowledge (and thereby to the theology of his three friends). Job now perceives that there is another way of knowing and speaking about God. His previous contact with God had been indirect, "by hearsay" through others (his friends, for example!); now it is direct, unmediated.

Job is now beginning to savor the Pauline "face-to-face" encounter with God in which faith, hope, and love abide, "but the greatest of these is love" (1 Cor. 13:13). This encounter brings the fullness of life to the believer.[8] Job therefore surrenders to God and can say with Jeremiah in time of crisis: "The Lord is with me" (Jer. 20:11), and with the psalmist: "I shall behold thy face in righteousness; when I awake, I shall be satisfied with beholding thy form" (Ps. 17:15). He can repeat here, after this meeting with God, what he had earlier said in hope: "My heart is bursting within my breast" (19:27).[9]

Yet the meeting has been a costly one. God had said at the end of the second speech: "Who will resist me and go away unscathed?" Job has learned the truth of these words, for he goes away limping from this confrontation with God, as Jacob did after his struggle with the angel. Limping, but content, for he has seen his Lord, and the revelation given to him has opened up a new world to him. He had hoped for this meeting and at bottom had always been confident that it would take place. At the worst moment of crisis he had exclaimed: "I shall see God; I myself shall see him" (19:26). This hope is now satisfied. Job has previously addressed God on various occasions in protest; now he does so in acceptance and a submission that is inspired not by resignation but by contemplative love. The encounter with God is a logical stage, given Job's attitude as a person of prayer.

Despite all his protests, Job has always been convinced of God's nearness and has always desired to draw close to God (see 10:8–9, 12; 14:14–15; 29:4–5). All the greater, therefore, was his affliction when he felt far from God. Nevertheless, the closeness he now experiences is beyond all his hopes: "Now my eyes have seen you."

4. The steps Job has just taken, the discoveries he has made, lead him to a conclusion ("therefore"). This verse is often translated on the lines followed, for example, by Alonso Schökel or the *New Jerusalem Bible:* "I retract and repent in dust and ashes" (42:6).

According to the majority of commentators, the general meaning of the passage seems clear: Job stands now as a creature before his God, as a child before his Father. His complaints and protests had in fact never outweighed his hope and trust. He does not now withdraw his claim of innocence, for his conviction on this count is as great as his faith in God. Nor does he have to withdraw it, for Yahweh has not repeated the accusations of the three friends. Neither does Job accept with resignation something he regards as unjust. God, however, has now made known to Job a plan and the meaning of a justice that cannot be contained in the straitjacket of the doctrine of retribution. Job, for his part, has come to see that his language had perhaps been disrespectful. He therefore repents and humbly proposes to do penance in dust and ashes.[10]

This interpretation is basically satisfactory and is consistent with Job's stubborn assertion of his innocence as well as with what Yahweh will say in the verses that follow upon the passage we are considering—namely, that Job has spoken correctly about Yahweh (42:7–8). Yet the translation of v. 6 that I have mentioned ("I retract and repent in dust and ashes") has always left an unanswered question: What does Job retract?

In point of fact, and as the majority of students of the book acknowledge, the verb translated as "retract" has no object.[11] The only alternatives, then, are to supply an object for "retract" and run the risk of altering the meaning signaled earlier,[12] or to look for other translations of the verb,[13] or to settle for a degree of ineptitude in the phrase for the sake of a general meaning that seems clear from the context.

It is of interest, therefore, to note here for comparison a new translation of 42:6 that was proposed a few years back and that I have made use of in translating the verse. The new translation brings out the rich consistency of the verse with greater depth and clarity.[14] The key to the new version is to be found in the meaning of the verb *naham*, which is correctly translated as "to repent." The author of the new translation points out, however, that when *naham* is used with the preposition *'al* it means "to change one's mind" or "to reverse an opinion" (see, e.g., Exod. 32:12, 14; Jer. 18:8, 10; Amos 7:3, 6). The text in Job thus means: "I repudiate and abandon (change my mind about) dust and ashes."

The phrase "dust and ashes" is an image for groaning and lamentation; in other words, it is an image befitting the situation of Job as described before the dialogues began (see 2:8–12).[15] This, then, is the object of the retraction and change of mind of which this key verse speaks. Job is rejecting the attitude of lamentation that has been his until now. The speeches of God have shown him that this attitude is not justified. He does not retract or repent of what he has hitherto said, but he now sees clearly that he cannot go on complaining.[16]

The new translation illumines the whole of Job's second response and makes it more coherent.[17] The Hebrew verb *m's,* "reject, repudiate," is no longer left hanging without an object; it refers, as does the verb "repent" (taken in the sense of "change one's mind"), to Job's attitude of protest and reproach: "I repudiate dust and ashes." This means that in his final reply what Job is expressing is not contrition but *a renunciation of his lamentation and dejected outlook.* Certain emphases in his protest had been due to the doctrine of retribution, which despite everything had continued to be his point of reference. Now that the Lord has overthrown that doctrine by revealing the key to the divine plan, Job realizes that he has been speaking of God in a way that implied that God was a prisoner of a particular way of understanding justice. It is this whole outlook that Job says he is now abandoning.

Many difficulties remain, but the horizon has been expanded. Job begins to see the way by which he is to go to meet God and others. This explains his gratitude and joy for what has been revealed to him in the debate with his friends and with God, and especially in the speeches "from the heart of the tempest."

Job's answer, of which the new translation just expounded gives a better understanding, represents a high point in contemplative speech about God. Job has arrived only gradually at this way of talking about God. At one point he had even felt God to be distant and unconnected with his life; he had then confronted this God in a bitter lawsuit. Now, however, he surrenders to Yahweh with renewed trust.[18] Like Jeremiah in a passage to which reference must be made in any effort to understand the Book of Job, Job might have said at this point: "You seduced me, Lord, and I let myself be seduced" (Jer. 20:7). Job truly believes "for nothing"; never before has he believed in such an utterly disinterested way.

We must, however, go more deeply into the meaning of Job's final answer or, more accurately, of the book as a whole.

BEYOND JUSTICE

What is it that Job has understood? That justice does not reign in the world God has created? No. The truth that he has grasped and that has lifted him to the level of contemplation is that justice alone does not have the final say about how we are to speak of God. Only when we have come to realize that God's love is freely bestowed do we enter fully and definitively into the presence of the God of faith. Grace is not opposed to the quest of justice nor does it play it down; on the contrary, it gives it its full meaning. God's love, like all true love, operates in a world not of cause and effect but of freedom and gratuitousness. That is how persons successfully encounter one another in a complete and unconditional way: without payment of any kind of charges and without externally imposed obligations that pressure them into meeting the expectations of the other.

We saw earlier how in the debate with his friends Job came to see that he must transcend his individual experience. The dialogue brought home to him that his situation was not exceptional but was shared by the poor of this world. This new awareness in turn showed him that solidarity with the poor was required by his faith in a God who has a special love for the disinherited, the exploited of human history. This preferential love is the basis for what I have been calling the prophetic way of speaking about God.

But the prophetic way is not the only way of drawing near to the mystery of God, nor is it sufficient by itself. Job has just experienced a second shift: from a penal view of history to the world of grace that completely enfolds and permeates him. In the first major step that Job had taken, he was not required to deny his personal suffering but to open himself to the suffering of others as well and to commit himself to its elimination. So in this second stage the issue is not to discover gratuitousness and forget the demands of justice, but to situate justice within the framework of God's gratuitous love. Only in the perspective of the latter is it possible to understand God's predilection for the poor. This special love does not have for its ultimate motive the virtues and merits of the poor but the goodness and freedom of God, a God who is not simply the guardian of a rigid moral order. This preference for the poor—Job now realizes—is a key factor in authentic divine justice. Consequently there is no opposition between gratuitousness and justice, but there is indeed an opposition between gratuitousness and a conception of justice that can be translated into demands made of God by human beings and that renders God prisoner of our deeds or our cultic actions. There is indeed a contradiction between the free, gratuitous, and creative love of God and the doctrine of retribution that seeks to pigeonhole God.[19]

Inspired by the experience of his own innocence, Job bitterly criticized the theology of temporal retribution as maintained in his day and expounded by his friends. And he was right to do so. But his challenge stopped halfway and, as a result, except at moments when his deep faith and trust in God broke through, he could not escape the dilemma so cogently presented by his friends: if he was innocent, then God was guilty. God subsequently rebuked Job for remaining prisoner of this either-or mentality (see 40:8). What he should have done was to leap the fence set up around him by this sclerotic theology that is so dangerously close to idolatry, run free in the fields of God's love, and breathe an unrestricted air like the animals described in God's argument—animals that humans cannot domesticate. The world outside the fence is the world of gratuitousness; it is there that God dwells and there that God's friends find a joyous welcome.

The world of retribution—and not of temporal retribution only—is not where God dwells; at most God visits it. The Lord is not prisoner of the "give to me and I will give to you" mentality. Nothing, no human work however valuable, merits grace, for if it did, grace would cease to be grace. This is the heart of the message of the Book of Job.

There is no doubt that in the period when the Book of Job was written, vagueness about any life beyond the present made the experience of suffering more intense and the doctrine of retribution less credible. But the Christian profession of faith in a future life does not essentially alter the point the poet was trying to make. As always in the Bible, the new and unparalleled fact of Christ brings a rupture but at the same time establishes a continuity. The poet's insight continues to be valid for us: the gratuitousness of God's love is the framework within which the requirement of practicing justice is to be located.[20]

This is an essential point of our faith; it is present everywhere in the Bible, and the Book of Job only emphasizes it in an extraordinarily forceful way. Human works as such do not justify, they do not save. St. Paul says, in light of the revelation given in Jesus Christ, that human works cannot tie God's hands. This is the point of his statement about "justification by faith" (Rom. 3:28). The faith that saves is itself a grace from the Lord. Entrance into the kingdom of God is not a right to be won, not even by the practice of justice; it is always a freely given gift. "By grace you have been saved," he tells the Ephesians (2:5).

As a fine passage in the Book of Judith makes clear, no conditions may be imposed on God. When the king decides that unless God comes to his aid in five days he will surrender the town of Bethulia, which is under siege by the Assyrian army, Judith says:

> Listen to me, rulers of the people of Bethulia! What you have said to the people today is not right; you have even sworn and pronounced this oath between God and you, promising to surrender the city to our enemies unless the Lord turns and helps us within so many days. Who are you, that have put God to the test this day, and are setting yourselves up in the place of God among the sons of men? You are putting the Lord Almighty to the test—but you will never know anything! You cannot plumb the depths of the human heart, nor find out what a man is thinking; how do you expect to search out God, who made all these things, and find out his mind or comprehend his thought? No, my brethren, do not provoke the Lord our God to anger. For if he does not choose to help us within these five days, he has power to protect us within any time he pleases, or even to destroy us in the presence of our enemies. Do not try to bind the purposes of the Lord our God, for God is not like man, to be threatened, nor like a human being, to be won over by pleading [Jth. 8:11–17].

This is a clear statement of the transcendence of God and the gratuitousness of God's love. Those who demand guarantees from God show that they have no understanding of God and lack the discernment (*bīnāh*) needed for comprehending God's plan (*'ēṣāh*). God is entirely independent of space and time. God acts only in accordance with the utterly free divine will: God does what God pleases to do. No love at all can be locked in.

The prophet Hosea is quite explicit about this divine love that operates independently of any human merits. When Yahweh's people ask forgiveness, Yahweh replies: "I will heal their faithlessness; I will love them freely" (Hos. 14:4). Because of this freely given love, God will always turn "the valley of misfortune" into a "gateway of hope" (see Hos. 2:15).

All this does not mean, however, that God does not look for a certain kind of behavior from human beings. As we know, faith finds expression in works, but these works do not become a claim upon God, for if they did, they would betray their own meaning. Paul's insight, so profoundly in accord with biblical tradition, into the gratuitousness of salvation and the mysterious, utterly free love of God gets to the very heart of the revelation given in Jesus Christ. Paul himself tells us that faith works through love (Gal. 5:6). The reign of God makes the ethical demand that every believer practice justice, but this demand is not in any way inconsistent with the free and unmerited initiative of God. On the contrary, it acquires its full scope and vitality only when located within this gratuitousness. That is why Paul is able to speak of salvation as unmerited and then sum up a little later by saying: "We are his workmanship, created in Christ Jesus for good works, which God prepared beforehand, that we should walk in them" (Eph. 2:10).

The justice of God is a fundamental datum of the Bible, and therefore God at no time rebukes Job for having demanded justice.[21] For God to reproach him for this would be to contradict the promise God had made to Abraham: "I have chosen him, that he may charge his children and his household after him to keep the way of the Lord by doing righteousness and justice; so that the Lord may bring to Abraham what he has promised him" (Gen. 18:19). Nor can Yahweh contradict the act of liberation on which the covenant was based: "I am the Lord your God, who brought you out of the land of Egypt, out of the house of bondage" (Exod. 20:2). But in the just governance of the world God does not follow well-trodden paths that would limit divine action. Moving through history, God walks a path in freedom.

This freedom of God is a constant theme in the teaching of Jesus. It is, for example, the point of the parable about the laborers in the vineyard (Matt. 20:1–16). When the landowner decides to give a full day's wage to those who started work at the eleventh hour, toward the end of the day, his decision brings objections from those who had come to work early. The landowner tells one of them: "Friend, I am doing you no wrong; did you not agree with me for a denarius? Take what belongs to you, and go" (v. 14). The justice of God is not bound by the formalities of human justice. There is, then, this guileless expression of sovereign freedom and goodness: "Am I not allowed to do what I choose with what belongs to me? Or do you begrudge my generosity?" (v. 15). This is also the point of the parable of the prodigal son, in which the serious and obliging elder son cuts such a sad figure because he thinks he can confine paternal love within a narrow conception of justice.

But let me get back to Job. He has just been delivered from the envy that paralyzes reality and tries to put limits to the divine goodness, that leaves no room for generosity and, even worse, tries to take God's place. Yahweh, the God of life, has restored Job to a life that refuses to be imprisoned in a narrow ethical order but rather draws inspiration at every moment from the free and unmerited love of God. This deliverance is the object of Job's contemplation.

If the process of deliverance had not reached this point, Job would have retained a bit of the theology of retribution and, with it, a myopic view of God. The irony in God's speeches is, as it were, the scalpel that cuts into Job's wounded flesh and makes it impossible for the evil to remain and put forth new shoots. This critical juncture has been difficult and painful, but the result is worth the suffering. There remains in the world perhaps an obstinate residue of the unknown; we are still far removed from a completely transparent universe.[22] Job still has many questions, but the unknown is no longer a monster that threatens to devour everything, including his few and fragile certainties. The beast that is his ignorance has not vanished, but, like Behemoth and Leviathan, it is under control because of what he now knows about God and God's love.

It should, however, be evident that in rejecting the theology of retribution Job has not been freed from the necessity of practicing justice, but only from the temptation of imprisoning God in a narrow conception of justice.[23] He has been delivered, at least in principle, from the most subtle form of idolatry, a danger that has been mentioned at various points in the Book of Job. God is now seen by Job as completely free, untrammeled by the narrow theological categories in which Job had been trying to enclose God's dealings with humankind.

Job has learned from the Lord that the language the prophets use in speaking of God must be supplemented by the language of contemplation and worship. The point of origin for both languages is not so much a doctrine as a presence:

> Nevertheless I am continually with thee;
>> thou dost hold my right hand.
> Thou dost guide me with thy counsel,
>> and afterward thou wilt receive me to glory. . . .
> My flesh and my heart may fail,
>> but God is the strength of my heart and my portion
>> for ever [Ps. 73:23–24, 26].

God is a presence that leads amid darkness and pain, a hand that inspires confidence. Not all ignorance is dispelled, but the route is clearly marked. Luis Espinal, a priest murdered in Bolivia, wrote these beautiful and profound words:

Train us, Lord, to fling ourselves upon the impossible, for behind the impossible is your grace and your presence; we cannot fall into emptiness. The future is an enigma, our road is covered by mist, but we want to go on giving ourselves, because you continue hoping amid the night and weeping tears through a thousand human eyes.[24]

That is what Job did: he flung himself upon the impossible and into an enigmatic future. And in this effort he met the Lord.

Conclusion

The movement of the Book of Job is twofold: a forward, linear movement, and a circling movement of deepening insight into the answer to the opening question: Is it possible to believe in God without expectation of reward, or "for nothing"? In an effort to answer this question the poet comes upon the doctrine of temporal retribution. This, he finds, does not take into account his own experience or the experience of so many others. He therefore looks for a correct way of talking about God within the most strained and knotty of all human situations: the suffering of the innocent.

SONG AND DELIVERANCE

The Book of Job does not claim to have found a rational or definitive explanation of suffering; the poet is quite aware that the subject is a complex one. On the other hand, his faith prompts him to inquire into the possibility of finding an appropriate language about God that does justice to the situation of suffering. Not to make the effort is to risk succumbing to impotent resignation, a religion of calculated self-interest, a cynical outlook that forgets the suffering of others, and even despair.

Perhaps the author knew these attitudes from experience, for there are echoes of all of them in his work. But his profound sense of God and his keen sensitivity to the misfortunes of others kept him from yielding to these temptations. Despite everything, he remained resolutely disposed to look for and find a way of talking about God. He remains a deeply human and religious man who takes seriously the reality of unjust suffering and does not play down the difficulty of understanding it. His determination to seek and find—which is already a gift from the Lord—leads him through a battlefield in which, as one author puts it, the shots come at him from every side.[1] He does not avoid them, despite the danger that they may put an end to him and his hope of finding a correct way of talking about God. His personal courage and his trust in God impel him to follow paths that are a challenge to the theology of his day. At once more traditional than those who boast of being such, and more innovative than the standards of the mediocre allow them to be, the poet of the Book of Job is guided by God's hand to discover ways of talking about God.

We have followed these ways one by one. We have accompanied Job as his experience of unjust suffering broadened and he acquired a moving realization of the suffering of others. The ethical perspective inspired by consideration of the needs of others and especially of the poor made him abandon a morality of rewards and punishments, and caused a reversal in his way of speaking about God. We also accompanied him when after accepting adversity he rebelled and struggled with God but meanwhile kept hoping in God and, despite everything, finally surrendered to God's presence and unmerited love. But these two paths that we have traveled with him should not be thought of as simply parallel; in fact, they cross and enrich each other, and finally converge to yield a correct way of talking about God.

For Job to leave his own world and enter into that of the poor already meant taking the path of gratuitousness and not simply that of concern for justice. On the other hand, all prophecy has as its starting point an encounter with the Lord and the Lord's unmerited love (see the theme of the prophetic vocation in Isa. 6; Jer. 1:4–10; Ezek. 2 and 3). The result is that two languages—the prophetic and the contemplative—are required; but they must also be combined and become increasingly integrated into a single language.

Prophetic language makes it possible to draw near to a God who has a predilection for the poor precisely because divine love refuses to be confined by the categories of human justice. God has a preferential love for the poor not because they are necessarily better than others, morally or religiously, but simply because they are poor and living in an inhuman situation that is contrary to God's will. The ultimate basis for the privileged position of the poor is not in the poor themselves but in God, in the gratuitousness and universality of God's *agapeic love*. Nothing can limit or contain this love, as Yahweh makes clear to Job in the revelation of what Yahweh has established as the fulcrum of the world. Belief in God and God's gratuitous love leads to a preferential option for the poor and to solidarity with those who suffer wretched conditions, contempt, and oppression, those whom the social order ignores and exploits. The God of utter freedom and gratuitousness who has been revealed to Job can alone explain the privileged place of those whom the powerful and the self-righteous of society treat unjustly and make outcasts. In the God of Christian revelation gratuitousness and preferential love for the poor go hand in hand; they are therefore also inseparable in our contemplation of God and our concern for the disinherited of this world.

The doctrine of retribution contained a valid principle: that to be a believer requires a certain ethical behavior. But even this idea became distorted when inserted into a narrow framework of rewards and punishments.

The language of the prophets took a different approach in emphasizing the connection between God and the poor. It acknowledged the demands of ethics but it transformed their meaning, because the fulfillment of these demands was not regarded as a form of personal insurance or as a way of gaining a hold on God. Obedience was rather a matter of freely giving what we have freely received (see Matt. 10:8).

As a result, prophetic language supports and reinforces language inspired by contemplation of God. At the very beginning of the Book of Job and at the level of popular faith we saw the proper tone to be used in speaking of the

Lord's actions. But the tone weakened as Job's unjust situation was prolonged and as he listened to the criticisms of his friends. The language of mysticism restores vigor to the values of popular faith by strengthening them and enabling them to resist every attempt at manipulation. It thus prevents the distortion that turns these values into fruitless resignation and passivity in the face of injustice. But conversely the language of contemplation likewise becomes more vigorous and more community-minded to the extent that it is nourished by popular faith.

Mystical language expresses the gratuitousness of God's love; prophetic language expresses the demands this love makes. The followers of Jesus and the community they form—the church—live in the space created by this gratuitousness and these demands. Both languages are necessary and therefore inseparable; they also feed and correct each other. In a passage to which I referred earlier, Jeremiah brings out the connection nicely:

> Sing to the Lord;
>   praise the Lord!
> For he has delivered the life of the needy
>   from the hand of evildoers [20:13].

Song and *deliverance:* thanksgiving for the liberation of the poor. Contemplation and practice, gratuitousness and justice. This is a central theme of the Bible (see Ps. 69:34–35; 109:30–31). After her people had been delivered from the Assyrian threat, Judith sang a song of thanksgiving:

> Begin a song to my God with tambourines,
>   sing to my Lord with cymbals.
> Raise to him a new psalm;
>   exalt him, and call upon his name [Jth. 16:2].

The figure and theme of the suffering servant in Isaiah show numerous and very valuable points of contact with Job. In the first of the Isaian poems God presents the servant and describes his mission among the nations:

> Behold my servant, whom I uphold,
>   my chosen, in whom my soul delights;
> I have put my Spirit upon him,
>   he will bring forth justice to the nations.
> He will not cry or lift up his voice,
>   or make it heard in the street;
> a bruised reed he will not break,
>   and a dimly burning wick he will not quench;
>   he will faithfully bring forth justice.
> He will not fail or be discouraged
>   till he has established justice in the earth;
>   and the coastlands wait for his law [Isa. 42:1–5].

Anointed with the Spirit of the Lord, the servant has as his task to promote and bring forth justice (*mishpaṭ*) on earth, to restore the full justice of God.[2] A little further on, and in the context of the universalist vision of Second Isaiah, we are again urged to sing to the Lord:

> Sing to the Lord a new song,
>   his praise from the end of the earth!
> Let the sea roar and all that fills it,
>   the coastlands and their inhabitants [Isa. 42:10].

In this "new song" the text deals with *deliverance,* the melody adds the *thanksgiving.* Job likewise points to the combination of these two elements when he voices his hope that he will *see* his *gō'ēl* (his avenger), the protector of the poor (19:25–27). The poet of the Book of Job gives the name "Yahweh"— the guarantor of covenantal *justice*—to the God who "from the heart of the tempest" reveals to Job the plan of *unmerited love.*

Vision of God (final stage in Job's suit against God) and defense of the poor (a role he discovers for himself because of his own innocence) are thus combined in the experience of Job as a man of justice. They are two aspects of a single gift from the Lord and of the single road that leads to the Lord.[3]

For the same reason, emphasis on the practice of justice and on solidarity with the poor must never become an obsession and prevent our seeing that this commitment reveals its value and ultimate meaning only within the vast and mysterious horizon of God's gratuitous love.[4] Furthermore, the very building of a just society requires a stimulus and an enveloping atmosphere that gratuitousness alone can supply.[5] The point here is not to assign greater importance to the element of play and gratuitousness than to justice but to ensure that the world of justice finds its full meaning and source in the freely given love of God.[6]

The world of unmerited love is not a place dominated by the arbitrary or the superfluous.[7] Without the prophetic dimension the language of contemplation is in danger of having no grip on the history in which God acts and in which we meet God. Without the mystical dimension the language of prophecy can narrow its vision and weaken its perception of the God who makes all things new (Rev. 21:5). Each undergoes a distortion that isolates it and renders it unauthentic.

The journey of prophecy and the journey of contemplation are precisely that: a journey. The road must be traveled in freedom without turning from it because of its pitfalls, and without pretending ignorance of its ever new forms, for unjust human suffering continues to be heartrending and insatiable; it continually raises new questions and causes new dilemmas. It never ends; neither does protest, after the manner of Job. Although the way of talking about God has become clearer, it continues to be mysterious, as awesome and as alluring as ever.

Many difficult tasks remain to be done, many distressing questions to be answered; but an initial glimpse has been given of the path to full encounter with the loving and free God.

The language of contemplation acknowledges that everything comes from the Father's unmerited love and opens up "new horizons of hope" (Puebla, §1165).[8] The language of prophecy attacks the situation—and its structural causes—of injustice and deprivation in which the poor live, because it looks for "the suffering features of Christ the Lord" in the pain-ravaged faces of an oppressed people (Puebla, §§31–39). Both languages arise, among the poor of Latin America as in Job, out of the suffering and hopes of the innocent. For poverty and unjust suffering are in fact the situation of the majority in Latin America. Our theological reflection thus starts from the experience of the cross and death as well as from the joy of the resurrection and life.

This twofold language is the language that Jesus, prefigured by Job, uses in speaking of the Father's love. The author of the Book of Job stammers out what Christ will say unhesitatingly. He starts from the experience of unjust human suffering, which Jesus in turn will share on the "two sticks" of which Gonzalo Rose speaks to us with such tenderness. The author of Job reminds us of the call for justice that issues from God the liberator. The Messiah will make that same call his own as a central element in the message of love that sums up "the ten commandments of God," which fit into our hands "like ten more fingers," to cite Gonzalo Rose once again. The author of Job directs us toward that gratuitousness of the Father's love that will be the heart of the proclamation and witness of Jesus Christ. He seeks a way; he offers himself as "the way" (John 14:6).

A CRY OF LONELINESS AND COMMUNION

Jesus speaks to us of the Father, and in his discourses language about God achieves its greatest expressiveness. The Son of God teaches us that talk of God must be mediated by the experience of the cross. He accepts abandonment and death precisely in order to reveal God to us as love. Universal love and preference for the poor distinguish the message of the divine reign that both purifies human history and transcends it. Sin, which is the refusal to accept the message, brings Jesus to his death; the cross is the result of the resistance of those who refuse to accept the unmerited and demanding gift of God's love.

The final words of Jesus—"My God, my God, why hast thou forsaken me?" (Matt. 27:46; Mark 15:34)—speak of the suffering and loneliness of one who feels abandoned by the hand of God.[9] But when he cries out his feeling of abandonment in the opening words of Psalm 22, he also makes the rest of the psalm his own.[10] The whole of the psalm must therefore be taken into account if we are to understand the meaning of his lament.[11]

Psalm 22 expresses the cruel loneliness experienced by a man of deep faith. In the midst of this experience he turns to his God:

> Why art thou so far from helping me, from the words
>   of my groaning?
> O my God, I cry by day, but thou dost not answer;
>   and by night, but find no rest.
> Yet thou art holy,
>   enthroned on the praises of Israel [Ps. 22:1–3].

But in the Bible complaint does not exclude hope; in fact, they go together.[12] We saw this to be so in the case of Job. The confidence of the psalmist grows as he recalls that this is a God who has delivered the people of Israel from slavery and deprivation:

> In thee our fathers trusted;
>   they trusted, and thou didst deliver them.
> To thee they cried, and were saved;
>   in thee they trusted, and were not disappointed
>   [vv. 4–5].

The psalmist is referring to the deliverance from Egypt and to Exodus 3:7. This was the experience on which biblical faith was based. All the more reason, then, for him to describe his own pitiful situation in all its bleakness. This man who laments knows that God does not regard suffering as an ideal. His complaint is filled with a longing for life.[13]

> But I am a worm, and no man;
>   scorned by men, and despised by the people.
> All who see me mock at me,
>   they make mouths at me, they wag their heads;
> "He committed his cause to the Lord; let him deliver
>   him,
>   let him rescue him, for he delights in him!" . . .
> I am poured out like water,
>   and all my bones are out of joint;
> my heart is like wax,
>   it is melted within my breast;
> my strength is dried up like a potsherd,
>   and my tongue cleaves to my jaws;
>   thou dost lay me in the dust of death.
> Yea, dogs are round about me;
>   a company of evildoers encircle me;
>   they have pierced my hands and feet—
> I can count all my bones [vv. 6–8, 14–17].

The person speaking in this psalm tells of his misfortune and abandonment, but he says not a word of personal faults that would have merited such adversity. He is an innocent man who has been treated unjustly. This fact makes it easier for the evangelists to apply the text to Jesus at various moments in their accounts of his death.

The psalmist sinks deeper into suffering and loneliness. His situation is due to those who harass him and mock his faith in a God who can deliver him. But he remains steadfast; he knows that his God is bent on justice, and hears and protects the poor:

> For he has not despised or abhorred
> the affliction of the afflicted;
> and he has not hid his face from him,
> but has heard, when he cried to him. . . .
> The afflicted shall eat and be satisfied;
> those who seek him shall praise the Lord!
> May your hearts live for ever! [vv. 24, 26].

The God who could hear the cry of the Israelites when they were oppressed in Egypt does not disdain "the destitution of the destitute,"[14] the poverty of the poor and the least of human beings. Verse 26 is an allusion to Deuteronomy 14:29, which says that "the sojourner, the fatherless, and the widow"—the biblical triad used in referring to the poor and helpless—shall all "eat and be filled."

This solidarity with the poor and the starving, which leads to an ongoing transformation of history and requires behavior to this end, is the fruit of the gratuitous love of the God in whom the psalmist believes and hopes. This accounts for his self-surrender and praise toward the end of the poem:

> I will tell of thy name to my brethren;
> in the midst of the congregation I will praise thee:
> You who fear the Lord, praise him!
> all you sons of Jacob, glorify him,
> and stand in awe of him, all you sons of Israel! . . .
> All the ends of the earth shall remember
> and turn to the Lord;
> and all the families of the nations
> shall worship before him.
> For dominion belongs to the Lord,
> and he rules over the nations   [vv. 22–23, 27–28].

Jesus did not compose this psalm, he inherited it. It had its origin in the suffering of a believer, perhaps someone who in some way represented his people.[15] The important thing is that Jesus made it his own and, while nailed to the cross, offered to the Father the suffering and abandonment of all humankind. This radical communion with the suffering of human beings brought him down to the deepest level of history at the very moment when his life was ending.

But in adopting this psalm Jesus also gave expression to his hope in the liberating God who with predilection defends the poor and the dispossessed.[16] Luke could therefore put on the lips of Jesus not the cry of abandonment but words of confident self-surrender: "Father, into thy hands I commit my spirit!" (23:46; see Ps. 31:5).[17] He who has been "abandoned" abandons himself in turn into the hands of the Father. He confronts the forces of evil and sin when, in communion with the hopes of the human race, he asserts that life, not death, has the final say.[18] All this is part of the redemptive experience of the cross.[19] It is there that Jesus experiences and proclaims the resurrection and true, unending life, and becomes "the source of eternal salvation." Here is how the Letter to the Hebrews speaks of the value of Jesus' death for our salvation:

> In the days of his flesh, Jesus offered up prayers and supplications, with loud cries and tears, to him who was able to save him from death, and he was heard for his godly fear. Although he was a Son, he learned obedience through what he suffered; and being made perfect he became the source of eternal salvation to all who obey him, being designated by God a high priest after the order of Melchizedek [5:7–10].

Communion in suffering and in hope, in the abandonment of loneliness and in trusting self-surrender in death as in life: this is the message of the cross, which is "folly to those who are perishing, but to us who are being saved it is the power of God" (1 Cor. 1:18). Because it is "folly" it can pass unnoticed by those who have eyes only for wonders and manifestations of might. Paradoxically, this power of God is at the same time "weakness" (1 Cor. 1:25). It inspires the language of the cross, which is a synthesis of the prophetic and the contemplative and the only appropriate way of talking about the God of Jesus Christ.[20]

By using this language one engages in a "dangerous remembrance" of him who was publicly crucified at the crossroads and whom the Father raised to life.[21] This kind of talk—which the wise and understanding of this world regard as madness—calls all human beings together "as a church" via the privileged choice of the weak and despised of human history.

> For consider your call, brethren; not many of you were wise according to worldly standards, not many were powerful, not many were of noble birth; but God chose what is foolish in the world to shame the wise, God chose what is weak in the world to shame the strong, God chose what is low and despised in the world, even things that are not, to bring to nothing things that are, so that no human being might boast in the presence of God [1 Cor. 1:26–29].

At the same time, however, if we are to use the language of the cross we must have made our own the meaning of the crucifixion. Only within the following of Jesus is it possible to talk of God.[22] From the cross Jesus calls us to follow in his steps, "for," he tells us, "my yoke is easy, and my burden light" (Matt. 11:30). This invitation to follow him completes the passage on the revelation to the simple on which I commented in the Introduction to this book. At that time I singled out the message of the gratuitousness of God's love that the passage contains. It is in the context of this gratuitousness that the way of the cross to which Jesus invites us must be set.

All these considerations do not eliminate the element of protest from the final words of Jesus; they are rather an attempt to situate it properly. Even in his lament Jesus "spoke correctly of God." His cry on the cross renders more audible and more penetrating the cries of all the Jobs, individual and collective, of human history. To adopt a comparison that Bonhoeffer uses in another context, the cry of Jesus is the *cantus firmus,* the leading voice to which all the voices of those who suffer unjustly are joined.

"I WILL NOT RESTRAIN MY TONGUE"

This cry cannot be muted. Those who suffer unjustly have a right to complain and protest. Their cry expresses both their bewilderment and their faith. It is not possible to do theology in Latin America without taking into account the situation of the most downtrodden of history; this means in turn that at some point the theologian must cry out, as Jesus did, "My God, my God, why hast thou forsaken me?"[23]

This kind of communion in suffering demands watchfulness and solidarity. "Jesus will be in agony until the end of the world. There must be no sleeping during that time."[24] Commitment to the alleviation of human suffering, and especially to the removal of its causes as far as possible, is an obligation for the followers of Jesus, who took upon himself his own "easy yoke and light burden." Such a commitment presupposes genuine human compassion, as well as a measure of understanding of human history and the factors that condition it (consider the effort made in the documents of Medellín and Puebla to understand the causes of the present situation of injustice in which Latin America is living). It also requires a firm and stubborn determination to be present, regardless of the consequences, wherever the unjust abuse the innocent.

Human suffering, whatever its causes—social, personal, or other—is a major question for theological reflection.[25] J. B. Metz has, with refined human and historical sensitivity, called the attention of contemporary theologians, those of Europe in particular, to what it means to talk about God after Auschwitz.[26] For the terrible holocaust of millions of Jews is an inescapable challenge to the Christian conscience and an inexcusable reproach to the silence of many Christians in the face of that dreadful event. We must therefore ask:

How can we talk about God without referring to our own age? More than that: How can we do it without taking into account situations like the holocaust in which God seems to be absent from immense human suffering.[27]

It needs to be realized, however, that for us Latin Americans the question is not precisely "How are we to do theology after Auschwitz?" The reason is that in Latin America we are still experiencing every day the violation of human rights, murder, and the torture that we find so blameworthy in the Jewish holocaust of World War II. Our task here is to find the words with which to talk about God in the midst of the starvation of millions, the humiliation of races regarded as inferior, discrimination against women, especially women who are poor, systematic social injustice, a persistent high rate of infant mortality, those who simply "disappear" or are deprived of their freedom, the sufferings of peoples who are struggling for their right to live,[28] the exiles and the refugees, terrorism of every kind, and the corpse-filled common graves of Ayacucho. What we must deal with is not the past but, unfortunately, a cruel present and a dark tunnel with no apparent end.

In Peru, therefore—but the question is perhaps symbolic of all Latin America—we must ask: How are we to do theology *while Ayacucho lasts?* How are we to speak of the God of life when cruel murder on a massive scale goes on in "the corner of the dead"?[29] How are we to preach the love of God amid such profound contempt for human life? How are we to proclaim the resurrection of the Lord where death reigns, and especially the death of children, women, the poor, indigenes, and the "unimportant" members of our society?

These are our questions, and this is our challenge. Job shows us a way with his vigorous protest, his discovery of concrete commitment to the poor and all who suffer unjustly, his facing up to God, and his acknowledgment of the gratuitousness that characterizes God's plan for human history. It is for us to find our own route amid the present sufferings and hopes of the poor of Latin America, to analyze its course with the requisite historical effectiveness, and, above all, to compare it anew with the word of God. This is what has been done by those, for example, who in recent years have been murdered for their witness of faith and solidarity with the poorest and most helpless, those now known as "the Latin American martyrs."

"That is why I cannot keep quiet: in my anguish of spirit I shall speak, in my bitterness of soul I shall complain" (Job 7:11). Nor can the poor and oppressed of Latin America remain silent.[30] For them "day comes like a lamentation arising from the depths of the heart."[31] What the poor and oppressed have to say may sound harsh and unpleasant to some. It is possible that they may be scandalized at hearing a frank avowal of the human and religious experience of the poor, and at seeing their clumsy attempts to relate their lives to the God in whom they have such deep faith. Perhaps those who live, and try to express, their faith and hope amid unjust suffering will some day have to say humbly, with Job, "I spoke without understanding marvels that are beyond my grasp," and put aside their harsh language. Yet who knows but that the Lord may tell them, to the surprise of some: "You have spoken correctly about me."[32]

The prophet Isaiah announces that "the Lord God will wipe away tears from all faces, and the reproach of his people he will take away from all the earth."[33] Woe to those whom the Lord finds dry-eyed because they could not bring themselves to solidarity with the poor and suffering of this world! If we are to receive from God the tender consolation promised by the prophet, we must make our own the needs of the oppressed; our hearts must be moved at seeing a wounded person by the wayside,[34] be attuned to the sufferings of others, and be more sensitive to persons in conflict and confusion than to "the order of the day."

Only if we know how to be silent and involve ourselves in the suffering of the poor will we be able to speak out of their hope. Only if we take seriously the suffering of the innocent and live the mystery of the cross amid that suffering, but in the light of Easter, can we prevent our theology from being "windy arguments" (Job 16:3). But if we do, then we shall not deserve to hear from the poor the reproach that Job threw in the faces of his friends: "What sorry comforters you are!" (16:2).

In sending his Son, the Father "wagered" on the possibility of a faith and behavior characterized by gratuitousness and by a response to the demand that justice be established. When history's "losers"—persons like Job—follow in the steps of Jesus, they are seeing to it that the Lord wins his wager. The risks accepted in talking about God with the suffering of the innocent in view are great. But, again like Job, we cannot keep quiet; we must humbly allow the cry of Jesus on the cross to echo through history and nourish our theological efforts.[35] As St. Gregory the Great says in his commentary on Job, the cry of Jesus will not be heard "if our tongues keep silent about what our souls believe. But lest his cry be stifled in us, let each of us make known to those who approach him the mystery by which he lives!"[36]

This mystery is the one proclaimed by the dead and risen Son of God. It is the mystery that we come to know when his Spirit impels us to say "Abba! Father!" (Gal. 4:6).

Notes

INTRODUCTION

1. *Summa Theologiae*, I, 9, 3: "De Deo scire non possumus quid sit, sed quid non sit."

2. "¿Ultimo Diario?" in *Obras Completas* (Lima: Horizonte, 1983), 5:197.

3. E. Jüngel, *Dio mistero del mundo* (Brescia: Queriniana, 1982), 328.

4. On this subject, see J. Dupont, *Les Béatitudes* (Paris: Gabalda, 1969), 2:198–204.

5. As is well known, this idea was expressed in the *Aporte del Conferencia episcopal peruana al documento de consulta del CELAM para la tercera conferencia general del episcopado latinoamericano* (Lima, 1978), n. 4. 2. 1.

6. See G. Gutiérrez, *A Theology of Liberation: History, Politics and Salvation* (Maryknoll, N.Y.: Orbis, 1973), pp. 11–13.

7. I take these points from my book, *El Dios de la Vida* (Lima: Departamento de Teología de la Universidad Católica, 1982), pp. 6–9.

8. I am thinking of theologies that spring from divergent racial and cultural situations—for example, those based on the situation of women. For the feminist perspective in theology, see the major work of Elisabeth Schüssler Fiorenza, *In Memory of Her: A Feminist Theological Reconstruction of Christian Origins* (New York: Crossroad, 1983).

9. "The Theology of Liberation in Africa," in Kofi Appiah-Kubi and Sergio Torres, eds., *African Theology en Route: Papers from the Pan-African Conference of Third World Theologians, December 17–23, 1977, Accra, Ghana* (Maryknoll, N.Y.: Orbis, 1979), p. 163. This was the problem that James Cone raised with regard to God at the very beginning of the black theology of liberation; see his *God of the Oppressed* (New York: Seabury, 1975).

10. "Le problème du mal, problème de société," in *Théologie de la libération* (Louvain-la-Neuve: Annales Cardijn, 1985), p. 33. According to Gesché, "our Christian theology has two traditions on evil: one I shall call 'Pauline' (or 'Augustinian'), the other 'Lukan' " (p. 30). The first of the two traditions focuses on moral evil that is deliberately caused by the responsible person. The other focuses on evil that is suffered by the innocent and involves more than the individual; it is physical evil, the evil of misfortune. For an example of innocent suffering, Gesché appeals to the Lukan parable of the Good Samaritan: the injured man at the roadside does not merit the misfortune that has befallen him. The point is well taken, but the man's innocence does not relieve the highwaymen of their responsibility—although the determination of this responsibility (and seeking out a fitting punishment) is in no way a prior condition that must be met for the Samaritan to approach the man who has been mistreated. In this case, the innocence present in the suffering refers to the injured man, not to the evildoers.

11. F. Guamán Poma de Ayala, *El primer Nueva Coronica y Buen Gobierno* (Mexico City: Siglo XXI, 1980), 3:1105, 1102, and 1104.

105

12. Tutu, "Theology," p. 163.

13. Guamán Poma, *Nueva Coronica*, 3:903.

14. This and the other passages of Arguedas that I shall cite are taken from chap. 1, "El Viejo" ("The Old Man"), of his novel, *Los Ríos Profundos* (Obras Completas, vol. 3, Lima: Horizonte, 1983); Engl. trans., *Deep Rivers* (Austin: University of Texas Press, 1978), pp. 3–23. This tightly knit and beautifully written chapter sketches the contrast that is the key to the entire novel: between the *pongo* ("Hacienda Indians who are obliged to take turns working as unpaid servants in the landowner's house"), who resembles Christ, and the Old Man ("the Antichrist," who is a miser like "all the gentry of Cuzco"). See P. Trigo, *Arguedas: Mito, historia y religión,* and G. Gutiérrez, *Entre las calandrias* (Lima: CEP, 1982).

15. The city of Cuzco both attracts and repels Ernesto; this ancient capital of the empire is today a center of oppression of Amerindians and the residence of covetous, exploitive masters whose religion is hypocritical. A little further on from the passage I have just cited in the text, Ernesto says: "The visage of the Christ, the voice of the big bell, the perpetually frightened expression of the *pongo*, and the Old Man on his knees in the cathedral, even the silence of the Loreto Quijllu depressed me. Nowhere else must human beings suffer so much as here" (p. 20).

16. See Ignacio Ellacuría, "El pueblo crucificado," in *Cruz y Resurrección* (Mexico City: CRT, 1978), p. 49: "This phrase sums up the existence of a great part of the human race that has been literally and historically crucified by natural disasters and, above all, by oppression inflicted by other human beings at the historical level. The situation awakens in the Christian soul an unavoidable question that includes many others: What meaning does this historical reality—the oppression of the majority of the race—have for and in the history of salvation?" See also Leonardo Boff, *Paixão de Cristo—paixão do mundo* (Petrópolis: Vozes, 1978; Engl. trans., *Passion of Christ, Passion of the World* [Maryknoll, N.Y.: Orbis, forthcoming]), and Jon Sobrino, "El resucitado es el crucificado. Lectura de la resurrección de Jesús desde los crucificados del mundo," in *Jesús en América Latina* (Santander: Sal Terrae, 1982).

17. "Historia de la Indias," in his *Obras Escogidas* (Madrid: Biblioteca de Autores Cristianos, 1957), 2:511.

18. See G. Gutiérrez, *Beber en su propio pozo* (Lima: CEP, 1983); Engl. trans., *We Drink from Our Own Wells: The Spiritual Journey of a People* (Maryknoll, N.Y.: Orbis, 1984), p. 34.

19. In his outstanding recent commentary, *The Book of Job* (Philadelphia: Westminster, 1985), N. C. Habel says: "No exegete can gain complete mastery of a text which is so complex and unclear at many points. No critic can do complete justice to the enormous volume of exegetical comment and textual emendation associated with the book of Job in a commentary of this length. Nor can all of the numerous contemporary and ancient techniques of interpreting a biblical text be explored fully in connection with each unit of analysis" (p. 9). Habel's commentary is 586 pages long!

20. This fact has at times caused me to go into some details of the book and to make some points of a technical kind; I have tried as far as possible to put these discussions into the footnotes so as not to overload the text.

21. See G. Gutiérrez, *The Power of the Poor in History* (Maryknoll, N.Y.: Orbis, 1983), pp. 103–4, and *Beber en su propio pozo* (Lima: CEP, rev. and enlarged ed., Lima: CEP, 1983), p. 204. G. Múgica, "El método teológico: una cuestión de espiritualidad," in *Vida y reflexión* (Lima: CEP, 1983), rightly remarks: "Spirituality is the principal key for understanding and establishing in detail the method proper to the theology of

liberation" (p. 22). In the same volume, see R. McAfee Brown, "Espiritualidad y liberación" (pp. 165–78).

22. Bibliography on the Book of Job is abundant. The notes of this book will give references to and remarks on the important exegetical studies I have read with close attention and with profit for my reflections.

23. For some aspects of thought about God in Latin American theology, see Victorio Araya, *El Dios de los pobres* (San José, Costa Rica: Ed. SEBILA, 1983); Engl. trans., *The God of the Poor* (Maryknoll, N.Y.: Orbis, 1987).

24. *Church Dogmatics*, IV/3, part 1 (Edinburgh: T. and T. Clark, 1961), p. 384.

PART I, INTRODUCTION

1. The common view is that the sections in prose are essentially an old story of a popular kind ("There was a man . . ."—1:1), which the author of the Book of Job found and divided into two parts to enclose the poetic section, which is his own. (This view was proposed over twenty-five years ago by a specialist on Job; see G. Fohrer, *Introduction to the Old Testament* [Nashville: Abingdon, 1970], p. 325.) The question of the extent to which the poet may have revised the old story to make it fit his purpose is still an open one; there is not enough evidence to justify a hard and fast position. J. L. Sicre gives a critical survey of opinions on the subject in L. Alonso Schökel and J. L. Sicre, *Job. Comentario teológico y literario* (Madrid: Cristiandad, 1983), pp. 36–43.

The date of the composition of the book is also debated. There is agreement today that it was written between 500 and 350 B.C., probably in the province of Judea. This places it in the period after the Babylonian exile, a painful experience that played an important part in the development of Jewish religious thought. See R. MacKenzie, "The Cultural and Religious Background of the Book of Job," *Concilium*, 169 (1983) 3–7, and Habel, *The Book of Job* (Philadelphia: Westminster, 1985), pp. 40–42. Habel expressly notes, however, that even if the period of composition seems in fact to be the postexilic age, the universality of the work is "far more important than the precise date of this ancient literary work" (p. 42).

CHAPTER 1

1. References to Job are simply by chapter and verse. [With a few explicit exceptions Fr. Gutiérrez uses the Spanish translation of Job by L. Alonso Schökel and J. L. Sicre in their *Job. Comentario teológico y literario* (Madrid: Cristiandad, 1983), which is based in turn on the version of Mexican writer José Luz Ojeda. Unless otherwise indicated, I use the *New Jerusalem Bible* for Job, the *Revised Standard Version* for the other books of the Bible.—TR.]

2. On these aspects of the setting, see M. Weiss, *The Story of Job's Beginning* (Jerusalem: The Hebrew University, 1983).

3. According to some, the author uses this non-Jewish setting (from the old tale) in order to avoid the criticisms that his bold theological views would otherwise bring upon him. The fact is, however, that even though the covenant is not explicitly named, it provides a backdrop for the narrative section and for the entire work. Its presence can be seen, for example, in the use of the name "Yahweh" for God in the prologue. For this reason, it does not seem to me that Job is to be regarded as a "holy pagan" (see J. Daniélou, *Holy Pagans of the Old Testament* [Baltimore: Helicon, 1958]).

4. Various names for God are used in the Book of Job. The name "Yahweh" is found

only in the prologue and epilogue and in the prose introductions to the discourses of God and Job's two responses. The name "Elohim" occurs chiefly in the prose sections. The archaic and poetic names "El," "Eloah," and "Shaddai" are found only in the lengthy section in verse.

Numerous hypotheses have been developed to explain this variation in names. Karl Barth, for example, thinks that "Yahweh" is the name used at key moments of the book: "Yahweh is the ruling Subject in the history of Job," whereas "Elohim" and "Shaddai" are simply predicates (*Church Dogmatics,* IV/3, part 1, p. 428). On the other hand, after a lengthy study of the question in his *Job et son Dieu* (Paris: Gabalda, 1970, 2 vols.), J. Lévêque sums up by saying: "In the final analysis, the problem of the divine names, on which so much has been written, is secondary as far as the theology of the Book of Job is concerned. . . . The three poetic names, which are interchangeable among themselves, are therefore theologically interchangeable with the name 'Yahweh' " (1:178). But despite this incisive judgment, the subject does not seem to me to be closed. Rather, when all is said and done, the poet's skill at slipping in themes and his subtle treatment of words and images suggest that there is material to work with on the problem of the divine names.

As a matter of fact, Lévêque modifies his earlier position in a later work. He explains that the name "Yahweh" is used in the prologue because at that point God's mystery is not threatened; in the dialogues, on the other hand, "the author prefers three other divine names—El, Eloah, and Shaddai—because they were more closely connected with the patriarchal epic and perhaps allowed a greater liberty of expression than the name given in Exodus would have" (*Job, le livre et le message* [Paris: Cerf, 1985], p. 13). The explanation is quite probable, but it does not exclude some other interpretations.

5. "The satan," instead of "Satan," because the Hebrew *hassatan* (noun with article) expresses the function of this character rather than his proper name. He is "the adversary," "the accuser," "the opponent." On his role in the Book of Job, see Lévêque, *Job et son Dieu*, 1:179–90.

6. In their Spanish translation Sicre and Alonso Schökel (n. 1, above) have *justo*; in this context I prefer *integro* ("a man of integrity") in order better to bring out the overtones of the word.

7. See S. Terrien, *Job* (Neuchâtel: Delachaux et Niestlé, 1963), p. 52: "The Hebrew idea of 'perfection' included both physical and moral health, and suggested wholeness, roundedness, homogeneity. A 'perfect' human being could be compared to a properly finished product. Job possessed not only interior balance and self-control, but was also a man adapted to his milieu. He was therefore 'upright' (*yāshār*), for he practiced honesty and justice toward his fellows. Integrity and uprightness were complementary virtues." See Lévêque's remarks in the same vein in his *Job et son Dieu*, 1:137–39.

8. R. Gordis, *The Book of Job* (New York: Jewish Theological Seminary of America, 1978), humorously remarks that "we have a Jewish Satan here, who answers a question by a question!" (p. 15). At the end of the book God will follow Jewish practice and answer Job's questions with questions of his own.

9. *Hinnām* means "without payment," "for free" (see Gen. 29:15; Jer. 22:13), and, as a derivation from this first meaning, "without a reason" (see Ps. 109:3; Prov. 3:30). Here in 1:9 the first meaning is obviously the correct one; in 2:3, on the other hand, the same word has the nuance proper to the derived meaning, "without a reason," "without cause"; see P. Federizzi, *Giobbe* (Rome: Marietti, 1972), p. 18; Lévêque, *Job et son Dieu*, 1:193–94.

10. Job will later see himself as one whom God has made a scapegoat, a typical object

of ridicule and contempt: "I have become a byword among foreigners, and a creature on whose face to spit" (17:6). In an article entitled, "Job et le bouc émissaire," *Bulletin du Centre Protestant d'Etudes* (Geneva), Nov. 1983, p. 20, R. Girard has revived a literal translation that emphasizes even more the paradigmatic aspect of Job: "He has turned me into the *mashal* [proverb, parable, laughingstock] of the nations, I will be a public *tophet.*" *Tophet* was a place where victims were sacrificed by fire after being spat upon in scorn (see 2 Kings 23:10; Jer. 7:31–32; 19:6–15). Girard writes: "The expression 'public *tophet*' signifies someone who is insulted, covered with spittle, and an object of public execration; it originated in ancient sacrificial rites." In this interpretation Job would be a propitiatory victim who is sacrificed in the name of the many. The Vulgate has *exemplum* for the Hebrew *tophet.*

11. I think therefore that Habel is right in claiming that whatever redactional stages the Book of Job may have passed through (and on this point we can only hypothesize), the work should be interpreted "as an integrated literary and theological work" (p. 21). E. Dhorme takes a basically similar approach in his classic and still valuable work, *A Commentary on the Book of Job* (London: Nelson, 1967), pp. lxi–cxi.

This understanding of the Book of Job determines the way in which the text is to be treated. Habel says: "This commentary treats the book of Job as a literary totality" (p. 9). I adopt the same view and therefore take the text as it has come down to us, neither mutilating it nor changing the order of passages in it.

12. This was still true in the time of Jesus. It explains, for example, why the cure of a leper (health of the individual body) is accompanied in the Gospels by a reintegration of the individual into society (health of the social body). In connection with the cure of a leper in Mark 1:40–45 and the Lord's instruction that the man show himself to a priest, Hugo Echegaray rightly remarks: "The cure necessarily has a double meaning: it brings the man a restoration of personal wholeness and it brings his resultant reentry into the body social, the recognition of him as an individual having full rights" (*Anunciar el Reino* [Lima: CEP, 1981], p. 35).

13. There is an echo of this view in Eliphaz's first speech:

> I have seen the senseless taking root,
>> when a curse fell suddenly on his house.
> His children are deprived of prop and stay,
>> ruined at the gate, and no one to defend them [5:3–4].

14. Dhorme comments: "Job sits on this heap of dust, ashes, dirt, which is found at the entrance of small towns in Palestine and is called the *mazbaleh,* 'dunghill' [or: garbage heap—TR.]" (*Commentary,* p. 19). Habel explains the meaning of Job s gesture by recalling the significance of ashes: "Job gives public prominence to his plight by sitting among the 'ashes,' which symbolize total negation and mourning (30:19; Gen. 18:27; Isa. 58:5; Jonah 3:6)" (p. 96). According to C. Westermann, the dominant literary genre in the Book of Job is the lamentation; only if this is kept in mind will it be possible to understand correctly the structure of the work. At the beginning of his well-known study of Job, *The Structure of the Book of Job: A Form-Critical Analysis* (Philadelphia: Fortress, 1977), he writes: "At the base of my investigation lies the simple recognition that in the Old Testament human suffering has its own peculiar language and that one can understand the structure of the Book of Job if one has first understood the language of lamentation" (p. vii). Job will abandon this entire outlook after God's speeches (see below, pp. 86–87).

15. The anguished solidarity in suffering which Job's wife displays (and which prevents her being regarded simply as an ally of the satan) was perceived in antiquity; see the odd passage of the Septuagint that is cited by Sicre, in Alonso Schökel and Sicre, *Job*, p. 107.

16. See Echegaray, *Anunciar*, pp. 26–27.

17. Léon Filipe, a poet of stimulating insights into the connection between the human and the religious, has a beautiful poem on the universal scope of Job's message:

> WE KNOW that there is no promised land
> or promised stars.
> We know it, Lord, we know it,
> and we go on working with you.
>
> We know that a thousand times over
> we will hitch our wagon anew
> and that a thousand times over
> we shall erect anew
> our old shelter.
> We know that for this we shall receive
> neither ration nor wage.
> We know it, Lord, we know it,
> and we go on working with you.
> And we know
> that over this dwelling
> a thousand times,
> and a thousand times again,
> we must perform the same old tragicomic trick
> without praise
> and without applause.
> We know it, Lord, we know,
> and we go on working with you.
> And you know, Lord, that we know,
> that we all know, all of us,
>   (Where is the Devil?)
> that today you can lay a bet with anyone,
> a safer bet than with Job and with Faust.
>   —*Versos y oraciones de caminante*
>   (Madrid: Visor, 1981), pp. 83–84.

CHAPTER 2

1. Job's bold language has understandably caused uneasiness and led at times to interpretations that try to moderate the tone of Job's protests; see, e.g., St. Thomas Aquinas in his commentary on Job: *Job, un homme pour notre temps* (Paris: Téqui, 1980), pp. 66–71. Fray Luis de León, for his part, writes: "If he grieves, he has reason to grieve, and it would be senseless for him not to grieve; if he complains it is because he is suffering, and it is natural for a sufferer to complain. And if he wishes not to have been born into such evil, I ask: Is there anything that compels us to choose life if that life must be spent so wretchedly? Who is in trouble and wishes to be in it? Or who is tormented

and wants to live in torment? Or who chooses to live a life of ceaseless dying?" (cited by L. Alonso Schökel, in *Job* [chap. 1, note 1, above], p. 120).

2. César Vallejo expresses this same radical experience in one of his poems:

> On the day I was born,
> God was sick,
> gravely.
> —*Los Heraldos Negros;* Engl. trans., R. Bly, ed.,
> *Neruda and Vallejo: Selected Poems*
> (Boston: Beacon, 1971), p. 219.

3. On the connections between Job's monologue and the Book of Genesis, see Habel, *The Book of Job* (Introduction, n. 19, above), p. 104. J. Vermeyleu notes "The darkness (*hōšèk,* Gen. 1, 2) is one of the major characteristics of the representation of chaos and the first act of creation is a rejection of the darkness, making the light shine (v.3), which is one of the divine attributes" ("Dieu et ses representations, antagonistes, dans le livre de Job" en *Qu'est -ce que Dieu. Hommage a l'abbé Daniel Coppleters de Gibson* (Bruxelles, Facultés universitaires Saint-Louis, 1985), 594.

4. A little further on, in his answer to Bildad, Job will repeat the same idea, adding the plea that he be granted a respite; little by little he will intensify this plea amid the hostility he feels directed against his life:

> Why did you bring me out of the womb?
>   I should have perished then, unseen by any eye,
> a being that had never been,
>   to be carried from womb to grave.
> The days of my life are few enough;
>   turn your eyes away, leave me a little joy,
> before I go to the place of no return,
>   to the land of darkness and shadow dark as death,
> where dimness and disorder hold sway,
>   and light itself is like dead of night [10:18–22].

5. L. Alonso Schökel (see n. 1, above) observes that in the first chapters of the Book of Job "*light and darkness* [is] the supreme question debated here; from this radical antithesis spring other sets of spatial and temporal contrasts" (p. 155).

6. See Dhorme, *Commentary* (chap. 1, n. 11, above), pp. clix–clxii.

7. In his article, "The Two Faces of Job," *Concilium*, 169 (1983), C. Westermann aptly notes that, contrary to what might be expected by the Western mind with its negative view of the complaint, the latter is here connected with prayer. But "when, in the Christian churches, the complaint disappeared from prayer, it spelt the end of this linguistic genre [i.e., in which the complaint had been part of prayer, part of calling upon God]." And he adds the perceptive comment: "Latterly, a change seems to be in the wind: some of the young churches are taking the initiative in restoring the 'complaint' to its rightful place in prayer" (p. 18). This, in fact, is what is beginning to happen in Latin America; nonetheless, the lack of understanding of the prayer element in the protest of the poor has not yet disappeared from among us. This protest—inevitably—finds expression in ways that perhaps are a challenge to mental laziness but that are seeking primarily to be faithful to the inspiration of the Spirit.

8. I think it worthwhile to cite the context of these sentences. In language whose

depth is comparable only to that of Job, Vallejo is here expressing his suffering but also, paradoxically, his hope:

"I do not feel this suffering as César Vallejo. I am not suffering now as a creative person, or as a man, nor even as a simple human being. I don't feel this pain as a Catholic, or as a Mohammedan or as an atheist. Today I am simply in pain. . . . Today I am in pain from further down. I am simply in pain. [Here follow the lines cited in my text.]

"I always believed up till now that all things in this world had to be either fathers or sons. But here is my pain that is neither a father nor a son. It hasn't any back to get dark, and it has too bold a front for dawning, and if they put it into some dark room, it wouldn't give light, and if they put it into some brightly lit room, it wouldn't cast a shadow. Today I am in pain, no matter what happens. Today I am simply in pain. I suffer, come what may. I am simply suffering" (Bly, *Neruda and Vallejo*, pp. 241, 243).

9. Guamán Poma, cited earlier, is a witness to this rupture. He describes in detail the extortionate demands the Amerindians suffered at the hands of different kinds of oppressors. He illustrates his report with a sketch of an Amerindian relentlessly pursued by six beasts. At the end of each paragraph in his lengthy, litanylike description of these vexations, Guamán Poma repeats with some discouragement: "And there is no recourse for the poor Indians" (*Nueva Coronica* [Introduction, n. 11, above], 3:656).

10. Alonso Schökel (n. 1, above) says of Job: "Beneath the despair, hope stiffens; despite everything, his uprightness looks to God for hope" (p. 193).

CHAPTER 3

1. The text says literally: "He has spoken the truth." The Hebrew word translated "truth" is *nekōnāh* (a synonym of *'emet*), which, according to Habel, "refers to what is correct and consistent with the facts (Deut. 17:1; 1 Sam. 23:23)"; therefore "Job's answers correspond with reality" (*The Book of Job* [Introduction, n. 19, above], p. 583).

2. See Gordis, *The Book of Job* (chap. 1, n. 8, above), p. 575.

3. See above, p. 6.

4. Echegaray rightly points out: "The faith of Job with its refusal of compromise and its lack of moderation is truer than the faith of his friends with its narrowness and conformism. In protesting against the injustice inflicted on him, Job is a much more truthful witness to faith in Yahweh than all those who 'grow accustomed' to injustice to the point of making it a necessary element in the system of human life. This is what has happened in the case of Job's friends and of God's false friends" (*Anunciar* [chap. 1, n. 12, above], p. 58).

5. Some students of the Book of Job think that this happy ending (doubtless part of the old popular tale that the author has kept) is a device the poet uses to end his work in a way that will soften the shock that the bold words of the dialogues may have produced in readers of his day. But I do not think it necessary to fall back on this subtle explanation.

6. K. Barth, *Hiob*, H. Gollwitzer, ed. (Neukirchen-Vluyn: Neukirchener Verlag des Erziehungvereins, 1966), p. 78; cited in Lévêque, *Job et son Dieu* (chap. 1, n. 4, above), 1:683, n. 1.

7. Camus, *The Plague* (New York: Random House, Modern Library edition, 1948), pp. 201–2.

8. Camus, *The Misunderstanding*, in *Caligula and Three Other Plays* (New York: Knopf, 1970), pp. 133–34.

9. See his *The Fall*, in which the main character, Jean-Baptiste Clamance, hears laughter while walking out one night and is compelled by it to review his life. In his case this means to review the answers Camus had given to the question that was his constant preoccupation: "Is or is not human life worth living?"

10. In focusing on precisely this situation I am far from, as Dietrich Bonhoeffer puts it, "trying anxiously . . . to reserve some space for God." As the reader will know, according to this theologian and witness we must learn "to speak of God not on the boundaries but at the center, not in weakness but in strength" (letter of April 30, 1944, in his *Letters and Papers from Prison*, revised ed. by E. Bethge [New York: Macmillan, 1967], p. 142). Bonhoeffer's worry was that if we start from situations of human weakness, we will reach a "God of the gaps" whose existence is required to compensate for human powerlessness, a God who becomes increasingly remote as human knowledge and power grow. Then "God becomes superfluous as a *deus ex machina*" (ibid.). Bonhoeffer's approach to the subject is responsive to the questions asked by the modern mind, which rejects a God who takes the place of human beings and refuses to let them live in an adult manner; see G. Gutiérrez, "The Limitations of Modern Theology: On a Letter of Dietrich Bonhoeffer," in his *The Power of the Poor in History* (Maryknoll, N.Y.: Orbis, 1983), pp. 222–34. When I speak here of unjust suffering I do so in a context different from that of Bonhoeffer. The question here concerns not weakness but innocence; not an undue control of God over human beings, but the way in which God supposedly works. We are faced with a human experience that seems to deny the justice and love of God. Is it possible in this situation to avoid seeing God as manipulative, to assert the Lord's presence in our lives, and to open ourselves to encounter with the gratuitousness and freedom of God?

11. In "Dios y los procesos revolucionarios," *Diakonía*, April 1981, J. Sobrino speaks in this context of a "Christian paradox" and cites the example of Bishop Oscar Romero who "precisely by defending living human beings gave great glory to God, inspired many Salvadorans to deeper faith in God, and intensified the life of the church. He effectively shattered the persistent idea that in the final analysis the defense of God requires a relativization of human life" (46–47). The same holds for the exploitation of human labor; see the Christmas 1975 statement of the Brazilian Catholic Worker Action, "Prohibido ser Hombre," in *Signos de Lucha y Esperanza* (Lima: CEP, 1978), pp. 105–6: "Living human beings are God's glory. To prevent workers from being full human beings is to act contrary to what God was affirming and bringing into existence through the death and resurrection of his Son."

12. See below, chap. 10.

13. This and the following citations are from Pascal, *Pensées* (Baltimore: Penguin, 1966), no. 418 (pp. 149–52).

14. I am not trying to limit Pascal to the themes developed in his famous fragment "The Wager"; I am simply pointing out the difference in perspective between Pascal and the Book of Job. The latter, I think, is closer to the experience of the impoverished Christian people of Latin America. In Pascal we have an exceptional case: the thinker whose mind focuses deeply on many and quite diverse human problems.

15. On the theological perspective suggested by the modern mind as well as by the "nonperson," see G. Gutiérrez, "Theology from the Underside of History," in *The Power of the Poor* (n. 10, above), pp. 169–221.

16. Westermann correctly observes: "In the figure of Job the poet shows the grave dilemma which may have to be faced if we are to affirm our belief in the God of the real world in the face of unintelligible and inexplicable suffering. We must take Job's

dilemma seriously, and if we are not likewise at a loss when confronted with the incomprehensible suffering of the world, then our theology is dubious" ("The Two Faces of Job" [chap. 2, n. 7, above], p. 22).

CHAPTER 4

1. In some very beautiful verses a little further on, Eliphaz says that this doctrine was revealed to him in dreams (4:12–17).

2. On the biblical roots of the doctrine of retribution and on its development, see R. Gordis, *The Book of God and Man: A Study of Job* (Chicago: University of Chicago Press, 1965), pp. 135–56.

3. [This verse is translated from the author's Spanish text.—TR.]

4. As A. Weiser, *Giobbe* (Brescia: Paideia, 1975), notes, "Eliphaz' speech is artfully constructed and is effective both rhetorically and as a piece of pastoral psychology. It has a wealth of profound ideas and of important and valid truths that will always be meaningful and that Job will find it hard to challenge" (p. 83).

5. S. Terrien, *Job* (Neuchâtel: Delachaux et Niestlé, 1963), says unhesitatingly: "In their view religion is a matter of trade, humility an insurance policy, and morality a coin that buys peace of soul and prosperity. On the surface, their creed is a magnificent one and their theism unblemished. Looked at more closely, their belief is not faith. . . . They are defending not God but their own need for security. . . . Their theism has become a subtle form of idolatry" (p. 41).

6. There are some who accept this view without question. Think, for example, of the expression so often found in biographies of the saints: "He (she) was born of poor but honest parents." The honesty has to be emphasized because (in the view of the writer) poverty is associated with thievery and other forms of criminality. Cervantes echoes this in a humorous vein when he says with reference to Sancho Panza: "Don Quixote made overtures to a certain labouring man, a neighbour of his and an honest fellow (if such a title can be given to one who is poor)" (part 1, chap. 6; Starkie translation).

7. See the remarks of R. H. Tawney (who refers in this context to Job) in his *Religion and the Rise of Capitalism* (New York: New American Library, 1963), pp. 199–200.

8. The sudden shift from the second person plural ("listen" is plural in Hebrew) to the second person singular ("you may jeer") seems to indicate that Job begins by addressing the three friends, but then speaks only to Zophar, who has just been speaking; see Dhorme (chap. 1, n. 11, above), p. 308; Alonso Schökel and Sicre (chap. 1, n. 1, above), p. 316.

9. Further on, Job will stubbornly repeat his stand: "I am innocent; life matters not to me, I scorn to be" (9:21 [translated from the author's Spanish version; NJB reads differently]). This assertion of innocence will become the deepest conviction of his wretched life: "Far from admitting you to be in the right, I shall maintain my integrity to my dying day. I take my stand on my uprightness, I shall not stir: in my heart I need not be ashamed of my days" (27:5–6).

10. The artfulness in this case is that of the serpent who offers knowledge without obedience (Gen. 3:1). In other cases, artfulness or cunning has a different and more positive meaning (see Prov. 1:4; 12:23; 13:16). On this point see Jorge Pixley, *El libro de Job. Un comentario latinoamericano* (San José, Costa Rica, 1982), p. 86.

11. Later on, near the end of the third round of speeches, Job will address Bildad in the same ironic vein:

> To one so weak, what a help you are,
>> for the arm that is powerless, what a rescuer!
> What excellent advice you give the unlearned,
>> you are never at a loss for a helpful suggestion!
> For whom are these words of yours intended
>> and whence comes that wit you are now displaying?
>> [26:2–4].

12. The translation here is that accepted by the majority of commentators. L. Alonso Schökel alters it in his and Sicre's commentary on Job. He makes the words a question and thus changes their meaning. Sicre and Alonso Schökel think that Job would otherwise be saying that in a different situation he would speak as his friends do; Alonso Schökel and Sicre find this unacceptable. But the argument is not convincing; moreover, to turn the statement into a question is to break the thread of the irony the author so often puts on the lips of Job.

13. In the story of the man born blind, the Gospel of John has a telling dialogue. When the Pharisees hear of the miracle Jesus has worked, they refuse to believe that the man "had been blind and had received his sight" (9:18). Despite the testimony of the man's parents that he had indeed been blind, the Pharisees suspect fraud and therefore speak harshly: "Give God the praise; we know that this man [Jesus] is a sinner" (9:24). "We know": they claim to know without having witnessed what happened. According to their interpretation of the law, Jesus is a sinner. For them, this is an established principle; *therefore* a miracle could *not* have occurred, and the cure of which there is talk is fraudulent. This is their "truth." The denial of facts is characteristic of abstract knowledge devoid of content. The reply of the man who had been the subject of the miracle is at a different level: he speaks in the context of what his life had been up to that point, and what Jesus had then done for him. He tells the Pharisees: "One thing I know, that though I was blind, now I see" (9:25). His knowledge has a source different from theirs; it comes from what he has experienced. Two kinds of knowledge are here contrasted: an aprioristic knowledge based on assumptions and prejudgments, and a knowledge that springs from experience and is straightforward and open to God's action.

CHAPTER 5

1. The poor in turn discover that they are one with Job in suffering and hope. Elsa Tamez puts it this way in her "Carta al hermano Job," *Páginas*, 53 (June 1983) 2: "The smell of death that is about you reaches our nostrils; we smell you everywhere. Your skeletal body goads us. Shreds of your corroding flesh hang from our flesh: you have infected us, brother Job, you have infected us, our families, our people. And your look of one who thirsts for justice and your breath that is soaked in wrath have filled us with courage, tenderness, and hope."

2. L. Alonso Schökel (chap. 1, n. 1, above) describes the passage as follows: "It presents a pessimistic triptych of a society divided into oppressors and oppressed. In the form in which the text has come down to us, the successive pictures or scenes form a montage of violent contrasts that emphasize the injustice of oppressors and the misfortunes of the oppressed" (p. 307).

3. After a careful study of the vocabulary of poverty in the prophets and the wisdom literature, John D. Pleins writes: "It is true that Job shares concerns with the wisdom

tradition, such as over boundary markers (Job 24:2); but the analysis of the socio-economic condition of the poor is more akin to that of the prophetic writers both in its thrust and in its use of terms for the poor. Exploitation is clearly the mark of poverty for Job" (in his as yet unpublished doctoral dissertation, "Biblical Ethics and the Poor: The Language and Structures of Poverty in the Writings of the Hebrew Prophets" [Ann Arbor: University of Michigan, 1986], p. 287).

4. On this point see the interesting observations of J. Pixley (chap. 4, n. 10, above), pp. 110–11.

5. In the midst of suffering, Job the believer turns to God and tells God of his bewilderment but also his trust. We find the same phenomenon in the religion of the people. "In response to the question, 'What does God do for us, and why does he do it?' a casual laborer, a migrant from the mountains, spoke of the contrast between his religious faith and the realities of his life: 'At times I feel as if he has forgotten the neediest; otherwise, how explain the terrible wretchedness of people's lives, especially in the barrios?' A workingwoman from the provinces was asked how God should feel when confronted with the injustice suffered by the poor; her answer was: 'Surely he feels humiliated; what I cannot understand is why he should allow it when he is so powerful.' But bewilderment is not the only response; to the same question about God's feelings a worker of Lima, a man from the provinces, said: 'God must feel sad that his children, who have the privilege of the gospel, leave their lands even though they know their claims are just; he must suffer from it' " ("La religiosidad popular en el Perú," J. L. González, ed. [mimeographed; Lima, 1984], pp. 47 and 50). See the volume published by the Movimiento de Trabajadores Cristianos, *El mundo de la clase obrera y el compromiso cristiano* (Lima: CEP, 1984), pp. 97–100.

6. A. Weiser comments as follows on this passage: "Job shows a clear awareness of the dangers of social division and a deep sensitivity to the wretchedness of the disinherited. . . . Is it not quite clear that in the history of the race the cry for divine justice is loudest when those disinherited by fate are forced to live in very harsh conditions without land or home, without food or clothing, and are compelled by need to steal a piece of bread or do something even worse?" (*Giobbe* [Brescia: Paideia, 1975], p. 277).

7. See chaps. 24–27; the text is not well preserved, and scholars differ on the correct order of various verses in these chapters.

8. Pascal, *Pensées* (Baltimore: Penguin, 1968), no. 512 (pp. 210–12).

9. The presence and meaning of this chapter in the Book of Job is much debated. Habel (Introduction, n. 19, above) gives a brief survey of views on the subject (pp. 391–92). In keeping with the approach he takes (the Book of Job is a literary totality), he himself maintains that the chapter fits in very well with the rest of the book. He thinks that the connection (which many interpreters point out) between the words "to shun evil is discernment" (28:28, in Habel's own translation) and the description of Job as a man who "shunned evil" (1:1) is important for the interpretation of the chapter, which he regards as the conclusion of part 1 of the book. "Thus v. 28 provides a formal closure which on the one hand is orthodox and traditional, but on the other stands in direct counterpoint to the poem which it precedes and serves as a deliberate counterfoil for the climactic protestation of the hero which immediately follows (chs. 29–31)" (p. 393). The contrast is due to the fact that the wise discernment Job is acknowledged as having was not enough to prevent his sufferings. "The poet thereby emphasizes once again that the traditional orthodox answer, while it may need to be said as a formal statement, is not acceptable to Job" (ibid.). Job will follow other paths to discover where wisdom dwells. According to Habel, "place," "way," and

"discovery" are the great motifs that give chap. 28 its structure (ibid., p. 394).

10. Dhorme (chap. 1, n. 11, above) calls the chapter "a general judgment on the previous discussions" (p. li).

CHAPTER 6

1. See J. Alonso Díaz, "Las 'buenas obras' (o la 'justicia') dentro de la estructura de los principales temas de teología bíblica," in *Fe y justicia* (Salamanca: Sígueme, 1981), pp. 13 and 18: "In their most common meaning, this pair (*mishpaṭ weṣedaqah*) contains a challenge to defend and advance rights that have been violated, especially those of the poor and the helpless—that is, the rights of those who have no means of promoting them themselves. The powerful already see to their own rights without help from anyone; they need no help. The 'weak folk' of the Bible, on the other hand, can never regain their rights unless someone helps them. . . . The God of the Bible, the God who has been revealed, is seen less as a *being* than as a *summons*; in God's action and summons, God is seen as *mishpaṭ*, an inexorable command of love for the neighbor in need." See idem, "Términos bíblicos de justicia social, traducción de equivalencia dynámica," *Estudios Eclesiásticos,* 51 (1976) 95–128.

2. I refer the reader once again to Guamán Poma; as we saw (Introduction, n. 11, above), the suffering and bewilderment that the situation of the Amerindians cause in him make him turn questioningly to God. But despite his complaints and protests, he does not forget that for the God of Jesus Christ "it is a good and holy thing to help the poor" (3:1106).

3. See Weiser, *Giobbe* (chap. 5, n. 6, above), p. 310.

4. It is difficult to determine the correct reading in v. 24; for this reason translations of it differ. The *New Jerusalem Bible* and Habel (Introduction, n. 19, above), p. 416, follow the reading of Dhorme (chap. 1, n. 11, above); Alonso Schökel (chap. 1, n. 1, above) does not follow it but regards it as possible (p. 425).

5. With justifiable enthusiasm, but also with a little exaggeration, Gordis, *The Book of Job* (chap. 1, n. 8, above), p. 348, says of 31:15: "The verse is a ringing affirmation of Job's conviction that all men, the lowest and the highest alike, are equal in rights because they have been created by God in the identical manner."

6. In his *The Prophets* (New York: Harper & Row, 1962), A. Heschel, who had a profound knowledge of the prophetic tradition of the Bible, wrote with reference to these passages of Job and Malachi: "Thus there was born the idea of one history. The particular event or situation is related to Him Who rules over all nations. Just as the knowledge of nature was born with the discovery of principles determining all happenings in nature, so is consciousness of history the result of an awareness of One God judging all events in history" (p. 170).

7. [Verse 18 is here translated not from the *New Jerusalem Bible* but from the author's Spanish.—TR.] Alonso Schökel and Sicre (chap. 1, n. 1, above), as well as other translators, interpret v. 18 to mean "from childhood he reared me as a father, and from my mother's womb he guided me," the subject being God (p. 437). For this reason they place v. 18 immediately after v. 15. M. Pope translates "From infancy I guided her." *Her* is the widow mentioned in v. 16; in this version Job is the subject of such guidance (*Job: A New Translation with Introduction and Commentary* [New York: The Anchor Bible, 1982], pp. 226 and 235). The text is difficult, but I follow the analysis of Dhorme, Habel, and others, and prefer the translation given here; moreover, it seems to me to be consistent with what Job says elsewhere in these chapters.

8. See Weiser, *Giobbe*, p. 322: "The measure of responsibility toward others derives from responsibility toward God, to whom Job will have to render an account when he 'arises' for judgment."

9. In connection with the passages cited (from chap. 29–31), Karl Barth speaks of "the striking social and even political aspect of the ethics" expressed in these chapters of Job (*Church Dogmatics*, IV/3, part 1, p. 386).

10. " . . . and covetousness, which is idolatry" (Col. 3:5); "Be sure of this, that no immoral or impure man, or one who is covetous (that is, an idolater), has any inheritance in the kingdom of Christ and of God" (Eph. 5:5). Terrien (chap. 1, n. 7, above) describes this passage of Job as a "pact against idolatry" (p. 210).

11. Gordis comments: "Job here repudiates the idolatry of wealth, which takes on two forms, trusting in one's possessions so as to feel free to act oppressively (v. 24) and rejoicing in the possession of gold, like a miser (v. 25)" (*The Book of Job* [chap. 1, n. 8, above], p. 350).

12. According to J. L. Sicre, *Los dioses olvidados. Poder y riqueza en los profetas preexílicos* (Madrid: Cristiandad, 1979), pp. 162 and 164, "the clearest statement in the sapiential literature of the choice between God and wealth is in three passages of the Book of Job. Despite their brevity, they are the most profound and interesting of all passages on the theme." He is referring to 21:14–15; 22:14–26; and 31:24–28. Of this last he writes: "When read in the context of the preceding verses, the passage also throws light on an important hidden factor: how to know whether or not human beings are putting their trust in riches. Beginning in v. 13 Job describes his past conduct: he has not denied slave or slave-girl their rights when they pleaded their case before him, he has not denied the poor what they sought, he has shared his goods with widows and orphans, he has clothed the naked, he has not taken what belonged to others, or exploited the peasants. In short, he has not sought to enrich himself or lived only for himself. He is therefore justified in saying that he has not put his trust in gold."

13. See the reflections on the spiritual combat in chapter 8, below.

14. Elihu is the only personage in the story to have a strictly Hebrew name. It is comparable to the name of the prophet Elijah and means literally "Yah is my God."

15. Many commentators are of the opinion that chapters 32–37 (the speeches of Elihu) are an interpolation; "the majority of commentators have no doubt that these six chapters were added later" (Lévêque, *Job et son Dieu* [chap. 1, n. 4, above], 2:537). They are considered to be either the work of the author of the Book of Job or of some later reader who was alarmed or angered by this bold and provocative document. L. Alonso Schökel, for example, thinks of a later reader as the source; he also regards these chapters as literarily inferior to the main chapters of the book. (The same view is to be found in R.A.F. Mackenzie, "Job," in the *Jerome Biblical Commentary* [Englewood Cliffs, N.J.: Prentice-Hall, 1968], 2:528.) In any case, as Alonso Schökel points out, the chapters are part of the canonical text. They are of interest to me in that they deal in part with my topic: the relationship between God and the poor.

16. For this reason W. Vogels describes the language of Elihu as "charismatic": see his article, "Job a parlé correctement. Une approche structurale du livre de Job," *Nouvelle revue théologique*, 102 (1980) 850.

17. I have already noted that the poet ironically puts on Elihu's lips words very like those of Eliphaz (15:2), which Job has mocked (16:2); see above, p. 29.

18. See Lévêque, *Job et son Dieu*, 2:574: "In the final analysis this glimpse of the

mystery of the divine *paideia* is Elihu's most personal and lasting contribution to the theology of suffering."

19. When Isaiah introduces the theme of the suffering servant, he breaks with the traditional doctrine that suffering is tied to sin. He assumes that human suffering need not be a punishment, but may have a quite different meaning in the plan of God. Gordis, *The Book of God and Man* (chap. 4, n. 2, above), p. 145, cites Isa. 52–53 and comments: "For the first time, the prophet affirmed the possibility of national suffering that was not the consequence of national sin, but on the contrary, a tragic, yet indispensable element in the process of the moral education of the race. For the first time the nexus between suffering and sin is severed. This insight of Deutero-Isaiah was destined to be deepened by the author of Job."

20. [These verses are translated from the author's Spanish text.—TR.]

21. [This verse is translated from the author's Spanish text.—TR.]

22. [These verses are translated from the author's Spanish text.—TR.]

23. In Habel's view (Introduction, n. 19, above) the function of Elihu's speeches is deliberately to create a climate opposed to "Job's expectation of beholding God in person" (p. 32). Elihu dismisses the very possibility by insisting that in the works of God, God has given human beings all the clues they need in order to realize God's transcendence and interpret God's plan in history. This is the point Elihu has been making for Job's benefit.

24. Some commentators see in 15:19 an explicit reference to the covenant: " . . . to whom [the ancestors] alone the land was given—no foreigner included among them."

25. Despite the difference in perspective, I think it well to cite the words of one of Camus's characters who does not have a clear grasp of the problem of evil but nonetheless says rightly: "I decided to take, in every predicament, the victims' side, so as to reduce the damage done" (*The Plague* [New York: Random House, Modern Library edition, 1948], p. 230).

CHAPTER 7

1. Here are some testimonies on this point. A peasant from the mountains says of the care God takes for us: "Like a father he takes care of us in the evils that afflict us, in our poverty and our hunger . . . but he also gets cross at us and punishes us when we do not seek him; he sends us rain and thus shows himself a father." An Aymara woman believes that "God always is; otherwise we would not be fed and clothed, and nothing would exist; we would live badly if we did not think of him" (cited in "La religiosidad popular en el Perú" [chap. 5, n. 5, above], p. 46). A person from the Amazonia region of Peru says: "God is good and lovable; he saves us and gives us life. We are friends when we approach him" (cited in the excellent book of J. Regan, *Hacia la tierra sin mal. Estudios de la religión del pueblo de la Amazonía* [Iquitos: Centro de Estudios Teológicos de la Amazonía, 1983]).

2. See D. Patrick, "Job's Address of God," *Zeitschrift für die alttestamentliche Wissenschaft*, 91 (1979) 268–82. The author thinks that in the speeches of Job he can identify "54 verses [addressed] to God in the dialog and four verses in his concluding peroration" (p. 269).

3. See Barth, *Church Dogmatics*, IV/3, part 1, p. 398: "The appearance of mature resolution suggested perhaps by chapters 1–2 was obviously deceptive. Job still has a long way to go before he will reach the point where we find him again in chapter 42.

With the fine sayings in 1:21 and 2:10 he has merely plotted the way. . . . He has now to tread it. What it means that Yahweh takes as well as gives, that evil is to be received at His hand as well as good, must now be experienced to the bitter end. The step corresponding to those fine sayings must now be taken."

CHAPTER 8

1. Nor is it foreign to the lives of the great saints. Here is an example that may surprise some readers. In this passage written shortly before her death, Thérèse of Lisieux speaks of the deep night, "the night of nothingness," through which she has passed: "Dear Mother, I've tried to give you some picture of the darkness in which my soul is blindfolded; only of course it does no more justice to the truth than an artist's first sketch does to his model. But how can I go on writing about it without running the risk of talking blasphemously? As it is, I'm terrified of having said too much" (*Autobiography of St. Therese of Lisieux* [New York: Kenedy, 1958], p. 256).

2. See G. von Rad, *Wisdom in Israel* (Nashville: Abingdon, 1972), p. 217: "No one in Israel had ever depicted the action of God towards men in this way before. Those who prayed the prayers of lamentation were not exactly prudish when they reproached God for his severity. But here is a new tone which has never been sounded before."

3. Numerous studies have called attention to the juridical language that the author often uses in presenting Job's debate with God (see, e.g., 9:32 and 13:3).

4. [Verse #35 is here translated from the author's Spanish text.—TR.]

5. It is always a profound experience to approach God and tell him how difficult it is to speak to him:

> How difficult it is, my Father, to write from the
>   viewpoint of the winds,
> so ready am I to curse, so raucous-voiced for song.
> How can I speak of the love, of the gentle hills of
>   your kingdom,
> if I dwell like a cat on a stake surrounded by the waters?
>   —Antonio Cisneros, "Oración,"
>   in his *El libro de Dios y de los húngaros*
>   (Lima: Libre–1 Editores, 1978).

6. [Verses 20–21 are here translated from the author's Spanish text. The translation is that of the Tanak as well.—TR.]

7. M. Díaz Mateos, *El Dios que libera* (Lima: CEP, 1985), pp. 38–39.

8. Vallejo voices the same complaint about God. Amid his loneliness, torn between envy and spite, he exclaims:

> God of mine, I am weeping for the life that I live;
> I am sorry to have stolen your bread;
> but this wretched, thinking piece of clay
> is not a crust formed in your side:
> you have no Marys that abandon you.
>   —"The Eternal Dice" ("Dados Eternos"),
>   in *Neruda and Vallejo*
>   (chap. 2, n. 2, above), p. 205.

9. [This entire passage is translated from the author's Spanish text.—TR.]

10. See the state of the discussion in Lévêque, *Job et son Dieu* (chap. 1, n. 4, above), 2:467–97.

11. See Lev. 25:47–49: "If a stranger or sojourner with you becomes rich, and your brother beside him becomes poor and sells himself to the stranger or sojourner with you, or to a member of the stranger's family, then after he is sold he may be redeemed; one of his brothers may redeem him, or his uncle, or his cousin may redeem him, or a near kinsman belonging to his family may redeem him." Num. 35:18–19: "Or if he struck him down with a weapon of wood in the hand, by which a man may die, and he died, he is a murderer; the murderer shall be put to death. The avenger of blood (*gō'ēl*) shall himself put the murderer to death; when he meets him, he shall put him to death." See the remarks of M. Díaz Mateos, *El Dios,* pp. 38–41.

12. "Thus says the Lord, your Redeemer, the Holy One of Israel: 'For your sake I will send to Babylon and break down all the bars, and the shouting of the Chaldeans will be turned to lamentations' " (Isa. 43:14; see also 41:14; 44:24; 52:3–9; etc.).

13. See the comparable remarks of G. von Rad, *Old Testament Theology* (New York: Harper & Row, 1962–65, 2 vols.), 1:415–16. J. Pixley (*El libro* [chap. 4, n. 10, above], p. 105), on the other hand, thinks that the context excludes any reference to God in this passage and that Job is speaking of some undefined "mediator." Ernst Bloch, in his *Atheism in Christianity: The Religion of the Exodus and the Kingdom* (New York: Herder and Herder, 1972), writes with complete confidence: "The friend Job seeks, the relative, the Avenger, cannot possibly be that same Yahweh against whom he invokes the Avenger" (p. 115). The whole direction of Bloch's interpretation of the Book of Job prevents him from accepting the identity of the *gō'ēl* and God: in his view, "Job makes his exodus from Yahweh" and turns to a secular world that is without God (p. 110). There is indeed something resembling an "exodus" in Job; it is not, however, a departure from God, but on the contrary a movement toward a fuller encounter with God. What Job leaves behind is the world of temporal retribution in which divine justice was imprisoned and rigidified; what he seeks is the universe of gratuitousness (see below, chap. 10).

14. [This passage is here translated from the author's Spanish text.—TR.]

15. Vallejo, *Obra poética completa* (Lima: Mosca Azul, 1974), p. 423.

16. "La de a mil," ibid., p. 67.

17. With regard to the identity of the *gō'ēl*, Gordis writes: "Actually, the problem arises only because of the tendency to apply Western categories of logic to the Oriental spirit. The sharp delimitation of personality is foreign to biblical thought. In all these passages, Job is affirming his faith that behind the God of violence, so tragically manifest in the world, stands the God of righteousness and love—and they are not two but one! Thus, Job's attack upon conventional religion is actually the expression of deepest trust. Hence Job is eminently worthy of God's final encomium pronounced upon him [i.e., 42:10]" (*The Book of Job* [chap. 1, n. 8, above], p. 527). Despite Habel's reservations about this position (Introduction, n. 19, above), pp. 305–6, I think that on this point Gordis is correct.

18. "I will flee from You to Yourself," wrote the medieval Spanish-Jewish poet, Solomon ibn Gabirol (cited in Gordis, *The Book of Job,* p. 527).

19. I join the majority of modern commentators in thinking that this passage provides no solid basis for an affirmation of the resurrection in Job; see Lévêque, *Job et son Dieu,* 2:479–89.

20. Alonso Schökel (chap. 1, n. 1, above), p. 284, points out how important "the use of the words *sar* and *zar*, enemy and stranger," is in this chapter.

CHAPTER 9

1. [These four words are translated from the author's Spanish text.—TR.]

2. These speeches have been the subject of widely varying and even contradictory interpretations. Alonso Schökel (*Job* [chap. 1, n. 1, above], pp. 532–34) briefly surveys a good number of opinions on the point; they reflect the bewilderment the whole matter produces in students of Job.

3. [This verse is translated from the author's Spanish text.—TR.]

4. Westermann, for example, writes in his *The Structure of the Book of Job* (chap. 1, n. 14, above): "One could almost say that the *fact* of God's answering gets overlooked in the consideration of *what* God says" (p. 105). In Westermann's view, "none of that [the content of what God says] alters the basic fact that God does answer him" (ibid.). In Westermann's opinion, the speeches of God have but a single theme: praise of the creator; that is why God's questions to Job are reducible to one: "Are you Creator or creature?" (ibid., p. 107).

5. See on this subject the penetrating article of Matitiahu Tsevat, "The Meaning of the Book of Job," *Hebrew Union College Annual,* 37 (1966) 73–106; reprinted in J. L. Crenshaw, ed., *Studies in Ancient Israelite Wisdom* (New York: KTAV, 1976), pp. 341–74; see esp. pp. 81–82 (= 349–50). Tsevat also gives a good outline of the different ways in which the speeches of Yahweh are interpreted (pp. 93–96, = 361–64).

6. There are no convincing reasons for cutting up these passages and getting rid of part in order to come up with a hypothetical single speech of Yahweh (see, e.g., Lévêque, *Job et son Dieu* [chap. 1, n. 4, above], 2:499–508, and Tsevat, p. 89, n. 50). If the sequence of the two speeches is interfered with, their message is weakened.

7. *Job et son Dieu,* 2:511. In the view of Alonso Schökel, on the other hand, *'ēṣāh* here has a broad meaning: "providence, including *nature* and history" (p. 552; italics added). But on the basis of a lengthy study, Lévêque is emphatic: "We will look in vain in the Old Testament for a text in which *'ēṣāh* clearly means divine providence at work in the government of the *material world*" (*Job,* 2:512; italics added). The point is important for the interpretation of these difficult speeches.

8. See Dhorme, *Commentary* (chap. 1, n. 11, above), p. 576. *Bīnāh* therefore plays an important role in God's first speech. God speaks of it at the beginning (38:4) and end (39:26), and makes other references to it throughout (see Habel, *Job* [Introduction, n. 19, above], p. 548).

9. [This verse is translated from the author's Spanish text.—TR.]

10. See Lévêque, *Job,* 2:531, n. 1, referring to Karl Barth's *Hiob* (chap. 3, n. 6, above), pp. 88f.

11. Tsevat ("Meaning," pp. 104–5, = 372–73) sums up his position in a vivid manner. He suggests that as an aid to understanding the meaning of the Book of Job, we construct an equilateral triangle at the vertices of which we place God, Job, and the doctrine of retribution. In the view of the author of Job, the three cannot coexist. Job's friends emphasize God and retribution, and eliminate Job. God's speeches eliminate retribution, and keep God and Job. This is also "all but" the position of Job who wavers, being unable to free himself completely from the doctrine of retribution. In any case, Job comes much closer to God than to the views of his three friends. "It is," says the author, "the limiting phrase 'all but' that makes a religious book of what would otherwise have been merely a theological treatise" (ibid., p. 105, = 373).

12. According to Pixley (chap. 4, n. 10, above), in 38:26–27 "we have a veiled self-criticism of Yahweh" who recognizes that there are defects in creation, in speaking of there being water where none is needed (p. 197). In my opinion, this approach misses the central message in God's speeches—namely, the revelation of God's generosity in the form of unneeded rain, and the joy with which God speaks of the creation.

13. Habel maintains that the "terminology common" to these two passages suggests that the poet deliberately intends this ironic contrast (*Job,* p. 545).

14. [This verse is translated from the author's Spanish text.—TR.]

15. Job has complainingly described himself as "companion to the ostrich" (30:29). On the God who sports with his handiwork, see Ps. 104:26.

16. See Lévêque's discussion of this theme with reference to Job (*Job,* 2:528–30). As the reader will know, this understanding of creation in contemporary biblical theology plays an important part in the theology of liberation; see Gutiérrez, *A Theology of Liberation* (Maryknoll, N.Y.: Orbis, 1973), pp. 153–60.

17. C. Duquoc, "Demonism and the Unexpectedness of God," *Concilium,* 184 (1983) 81.

18. [Verse 4a is translated from the author's Spanish text.—TR.]

19. In his deep meditation about Job, Søren Kierkegaard notes "The secret in Job, the vital force, the nerve, the idea, is that Job, despite everything, is in the right. On the basis of this position, he qualifies as an exception to all human observations, and his perseverance and power manifest authority and authorization. To him, every human interpretation is only a misconception, and to him in relation to God all his troubles are but a sophism that he, to be sure, cannot solve, but he trusts God can do it" ("Fear and Troubling" in *Kierkegaard's Writings,* Vol. III [Princeton: Princeton University Press, 1983], p. 207).

20. It takes several readings before the Book of Job surrenders its riches and allows the reader to see its underlying coherence. A superficial reader may think, for example, that in God's two speeches the same ideas are repeated. This is not the case; the two are related but distinct parts of a whole.

21. See also 38:3. In both cases "inform me" is literally "make me know." It is a barbed phrase that God takes over from Job, who twice uses it in addressing God (see 13:23).

22. According to Gordis, the reason for the presence of these two passages (38:12–15 and 40:7–14), one in each of God's speeches, that seem to have the natural world as their subject, is that "the identification of the God of history and of nature is steadfastly maintained in the Dialogues and underpins the Speeches of the Lord Out of the Whirlwind. Neither Job nor his Friends nor Elihu, nor God Himself is able or willing to 'solve' the problem of evil by making a dichotomy between nature and history, between the natural order and the moral order, between God's power and God's justice" (*The Book of Job* [chap. 1, n. 8, above], p. 561).

23. This is one of the passages in which Pixley thinks he sees God exercising "a self-criticism, though veiled by heavy irony" (*El libro* [chap. 4, n. 10, above], p. 196). See below, chap. 10, n. 21.

24. See Dhorme, *Commentary,* p. 618, and Terrien, *Job* (chap. 1, n. 7, above), p. 260.

25. See Habel, *Job,* p. 564.

26. See Terrien, *Job,* p. 260.

27. Many critics identify these two animals with the hippopotamus and the crocodile (that is how Alonso Schökel translates them—*Job,* p. 585). There are doubtless elements in the descriptions that suggest this view, but many other traits do not fit these

animals. Furthermore, the identification supposes a choice: that the author is dealing with real and not mythical animals (on this choice, see Gordis, *The Book of Job,* pp. 569–72, and Habel, *Job,* pp. 557–58). I prefer, therefore, to retain the names in the original.

28. Some scholars eliminate this part of God's speech. See Gordis, *The Book of Job,* pp. 122–23, for the arguments in favor of keeping it.

29. There are those who think that Behemoth and Leviathan are symbols of Job himself. Yahweh would be using them to warn Job about the consequences of his behavior; see J. Gammie, "Behemoth and Leviathan. On the Didactic and Theological Significance of Job 40, 15–41," in J. Gammie and W. Brueggemann, *Israelite Wisdom* (Missoula, Mont.: Scholars Press, 1978). Habel also suggests this (*Job,* pp. 559–61).

30. Alonso Schökel maintains that "if we stand off as we should and look at the four chapters (38–41) as a whole and keep their contents in mind, 40:7–14 stands out as the climax of the entire composition. In these verses God attacks the question head on, and not only the question but his rival in particular. To suppress these nine verses (6–14) is to end up with a different text; failure to recognize the central importance of these verses introduces a dangerous distortion into the perspective. We must read this short section as the summit between the two slopes of the discourses; these slopes support the central crest and thrust it upward" (*Job,* p. 572). The text is certainly important, but I do not think that the climax of Yahweh's speeches comes at this point, or at least not only here. The revelation of the gratuitousness of God's love in the first speech seems to me the essential point made in these discourses; within that all-embracing plan it is then possible to understand God's justice.

31. This distinction is quite different from that made by Westermann when he says that the first speech discloses the creator, the God of nature, and the second the Lord of history (*Structure of the Book of Job,* pp. 110–22). I think this is incorrect. The speeches of God form a unity and at the same time are complex in a way not captured in this view of its themes. Closer to the position I am defending here is that of E. Kissane, according to whom "the first [speech] has for its theme the Wisdom of God, the second, the Power of God" (*The Book of Job* [Dublin: Browne and Nolan, 1939; New York: Sheed & Ward, 1946], p. xxviii).

32. [Translated from the author's Spanish text.—TR.] The text of 41:2–3 constitutes the final words of God in the arrangement adopted by Sicre and Alonso Schökel; see their reasoning in *Job,* pp. 583–84 and 590–92.

CHAPTER 10

1. See Habel, *Job* (Introduction, n. 19, above), pp. 577–78, for a concise exposition of the various interpretations to which this text has given rise. The universality of the Book of Job allows a variety of interpretations; see, for example, the pages of Elie Wiesel on the significance of the book and especially in relation to the last words of Job. I disagree with his interpretation but I find it very captivating (cf. E. Wiesel, *Messengers of God* [New York: Random House, 1976], pp. 211–35).

2. [This line is translated from the author's Spanish text.—TR.]

3. [This passage is translated from the author's Spanish text.—TR.]

4. The word the author uses here for God's plan is *mezimmah,* not *'ēṣāh.* With regard to the former, Lévêque, *Job et son Dieu* (chap. 1, n. 4, above), suggests that, given the pejorative nuance the word has in other passages of the Bible (and even elsewhere in the Book of Job), it may signify here the interventions of God "in the lives

of human beings and especially the punishment of the wicked to which Yahweh refers toward the end of his [first] speech" (2:524).

5. Bishop Gerardo Valencia of Buenaventura, Colombia, once described this contemplative experience in very simple words: "Thank you, my God, for letting me feel your nearness. Allow me to improvise this discourse, having learned of you from you, like the children whose mother has them learn little speeches for her birthday. Allow me, then, God, my most loving Father, to hesitate and stammer, to put both hands over my face, to dash ahead and stop, complain, and end here" ("Los dos elementos," in his *Con Dios a la madrugada* [Bogotá: Tercer Mundo, 1965], p. 44).

6. Westermann makes an interesting observation at this point. "Wonders," which translates the Hebrew word *nipla'ot,* means "God's wonderful deeds for the benefit of his people or for his righteous adherents" (see Judg. 6:13; Ps. 9:1; 106:7). What is revealed to Job is not only "God's work as creator," but also God's "wonderful intervention on behalf of his people, the deeds of God upon which Israel's history rests" (*The Structure of the Book of Job* [chap. 1, n. 14, above], pp. 126–27). In the context of my own interpretation of God's speeches (which is not the same as that of Westermann, who regards the content of the speeches as less important than the fact that God speaks at all), I would say that Yahweh has revealed the plan of gratuitous love that embraces the whole of human history, and has asserted that this plan underlies all God's work as creator. This is the wonder that Job now recognizes.

7. As Pixley rightly points out (*El libro de Job* [chap. 4, n. 10, above]), if the intention were simply to recall the grandeur of God the creator, the references to this theme by Job, by his friends, and, above all, by Elihu would have sufficed (p. 191).

8. Miguel de Unamuno, a soul in conflict, gave vigorous expression to this desire for the vision of God:

> I want to see you, Lord, and then die,
> die wholly;
> but to see you, Lord, to see your face,
> to know who you are!
> Look at me with your eyes,
> those scorching eyes,
> look at me and let me see you!
> Let me see you, Lord, and then die!
> —"Salmo I," from E. de Champourcin's selection,
> *Dios en la poesía actual* (Madrid: BAC, 1976), p. 37.

9. Ordinary believers can have an intense experience of God's nearness. An Ayacuchan workman, for example, has said: "It makes no difference where we are, because we poor folk are with God our Little Father at all times; we never leave him for even a moment" ("La religiosidad popular" [chap. 5, n. 5, above], p. 53).

10. Dhorme (*Commentary* [chap. 1, n. 11, above], remarked long ago: "The only accusation which Job can level against himself is that of having discussed things which escape man's understanding" (p. 657).

11. See, e.g., Alonso Schökel, *Job* (chap. 1, n. 1, above), p. 593; Habel, *Job,* p. 576.

12. The *New Jerusalem Bible,* for example, has "I retract what I have said." The object here ("what I have said") is not in the text but has been added for the sake of coherence. M. Pope (*Job,* pp. 348–49) thinks that it is "doubtless the correct interpreta-

tion" because "when the object of the verb is fear from the context, it does not need to be expressed."

13. Some critics give other translations of the verb here rendered as "retract" (in Hebrew *m's,* literally, "repudiate, reject"). Thus the (French) *Traduction Oecumenique de la Bible* (*TOB*) has "I abhor myself."

14. Dale Patrick, "The Translation of Job XLII, 6," *Vetus Testamentum,* 26 (1976) 369–71; see also the article of Patrick that was cited above in note 2, chap. 7. I should note that in his essays Patrick adopts Westermann's view of the importance of the language of lamentation in the Book of Job (see above, note 14, chap. 1).

15. See n. 14, above, on this passage. Habel, who gives his authoritative endorsement to Patrick's translation, observes that in the Book of Job "the author's literary technique of balancing narrative features at the beginning and end of the plot suggests that the 'dust and ashes' here refer back to episodes in the prologue where Job separated himself from the community by sitting among the ashes (2:8) and where his friends expressed sympathy with his flight by flinging dust into the air (2:12). 'Dust and ashes' therefore seem to represent the status and role of Job as isolated sufferer and humiliated litigant" (*Job,* p. 583).

16. Patrick comments on "Job's intention of abandoning the posture of mourning" ("Translation," p. 371). In his later article, "Job's Address of God" (see above, chap. 7, n. 2), Patrick says more specifically: "Job does not repudiate what he said before or express remorse. Rather, he acknowledges the wonders of Yahweh's ways and declares that he will change, because of God's address, his speech from accusation and lament to praise and rejoicing" (p. 281).

17. L. Kaplan, "Maimonides, Dale Patrick, and Job XLII, 6," *Vetus Testamentum,* 28 (1978) 356–58, has pointed out, moreover, that this translation is not new. Eight centuries ago, the Jewish philosopher Maimonides translated the verse in the same way in his well-known *Guide of the Perplexed.*

18. Allow me to cite Vallejo once more. He too brought suit against God because of the sufferings he endured. But he too was able to meet God and enjoy God's presence with tenderness—and with almost condescending understanding:

> I feel that God is traveling
> so much in me, with the dark and the sea.
> With him we go along together. It is getting dark.
> With him we get dark. All orphans. . . .
>
> But I feel God. And it even seems
> that he sets aside some good color for me.
> He is kind and sad, like those who care for the sick;
> he whispers with sweet contempt like a lover's:
> his heart must give him great pain.
> —"God" ("Dios"), in *Neruda and Vallejo*
> (chap. 2, n. 2 above), p. 209.

19. Tsevat ("Meaning" [chap. 9, n. 5, above] perceptively indicates the role that the doctrine of retribution plays in God's answer and therefore in the meaning of the Book of Job. He writes: "Only the elimination of the doctrine of retribution can solve the problem of the book" (p. 8, = 366). But in his view this means doing away with the error of believing that "the world is founded on justice" (p. 97, = 365). In other words, he

seems to identify justice and retribution, so that to do away with the second is to do away with the first as well. Going a step further, Tsevat claims that in the speeches God is telling Job: "Divine justice is not an element of reality. It is a figment existing only in the misguided philosophy with which you have been inculcated. The world in which you and your friends are spun is a dream. Wake up, Job!" And, he says, "wake up is what Job does at the end" (p. 100, = 368). In Tsevat's view, "justice is not woven into the texture of the universe nor is God occupied with its administration." This does not, however, excuse "man from his obligations to establish justice on earth"; justice remains "an ideal to be realized by society and in it" (p. 104, = 372).

Tsevat does not give us any justification for this requirement of establishing justice (he mentions the requirement only in passing). And in fact, after what he has said, it would be difficult to provide any justification, especially one that has a basis in God. His work as a whole shows subtle analysis, insights into various aspects of the Book of Job, and a sense of God's transcendence (though he never speaks explicitly of the *gratuitousness* of God's love). I think, however, that he creates a gap between God and justice; he leaves the latter—and commitment to the poor—unconnected with our relationship with the Lord. Using the language of the present book, I would say that I sense in Tsevat's work a serious lack of the prophetic dimension that talk about God must have.

20. Terrien (*Job* [chap. 1, n. 7, above]) says of the Book of Job as a whole: "The Book takes its place with the prophets and the psalms at the very heart of Hebraic theology; at times, like those others, it transcends the limitations of the Old Testament. The poet of *Job* avoids the particularism of race, the Law, ritual, and even the covenant, and gives us the poetry of pure religion" (p. 49). I agree fully with Terrien's insistence on highlighting the message of God's gratuitous love in the Book of Job, but I miss in his commentary (as in that of Tsevat) an appreciation of the requirement of doing justice as a way of knowing and speaking of God.

21. Tsevat does not seem to me to be correct when he concludes his analysis of Job's rejection of retribution by saying: "He Who speaks to man in the Book of Job is neither a just nor an unjust god but God" ("Meaning," p. 105, = 373). P. Federizzi, *Giobbe* (Rome: Marietti, 1972), adopts the same position: "He is neither just nor unjust; he is God" (p. 284). The desire to safeguard the transcendence of God (or discouragement at the complexity of the book's message) cannot justify such a claim. As Gordis very properly says: "A God without justice is no God to an ancient Hebrew" (*The Book of God and Man* [chap. 4, n. 2, above], p. 127). A careful analysis of the book as a whole and in particular of God's speeches clearly shows the importance of the theme of divine justice in the work. The rejection of the doctrine of retribution and the strong assertion of the gratuitousness of God's love not only do not exclude or render meaningless the call for justice; rather they reaffirm it and locate it in its proper context. I regard this as a central point in the interpretation of the Book of Job.

22. It is this presence of the incomprehensible that gives rise to the tragic sense of human existence, a favorite theme in Greek culture. Paul Ricoeur interprets the Book of Job in this perspective in his *The Symbolism of Evil* (New York: Harper & Row, 1967): "As in tragedy, the final theophany has explained nothing to him [Job], but it has changed his view; he is ready to identify his freedom with inimical necessity; he is ready to convert freedom and necessity into fate" (p. 321). I do think that there is an element of tragedy in the book but God's self-revelation has given content to Job's thinking and joy—amid suffering—to his life.

23. Pixley takes some of Tsevat's ideas as his starting point, but in the end his

interpretation stresses aspects that almost contradict the emphases in Tsevat. As I have already pointed out, in Pixley's view God's speeches show God to be self-critical and critical of creation. "The irony that the author [of the Book of Job] employs in this section paves the way for the resolution in which he admits the validity of Job's attacks on God's justice" (*El libro,* p. 192; Gordis, in his *The Book of Job* [chap. 1, n. 8, above], pp. 561 and 566, takes a similar approach to the interpretation of 40:7–14). What we have here, says Pixley, is "the self-criticism of a God who has become aware of his own limitations" (p. 203). He thus agrees that Job is right, and he is therefore "wholeheartedly ashamed of Job for continuing to debate his case" (p. 205). In fact, "Job has failed to understand that even mighty Yahweh has problems in governing the world justly. Job has not grasped the implications of God's historicity" (p. 213). This explains Job's final acceptance once he realizes that "his search for complete justification in this world was a mistaken one, because not everything in this world is justifiable" (ibid.). Job's repentance refers to this misunderstanding. The result of God's self-criticism is to call upon Job to help God in the historical task of establishing an authentic justice on earth. "Job has discovered that the problem of injustice is not theoretical but practical, and therefore he changes his strategy. . . . The solution is to be found within history, as God and Job together take part in the transformation of the world so that this kind of thing will not be repeated" (pp. 214 and 217). (Pixley has repeated his interpretation in "Jó, ou diálogo sobre a razão teológica," *Perspectiva Teológica,* 40 [1984] 333–43).

There are some interesting points in this provocative interpretation, but I have already indicated my disagreement with it. The task of establishing justice is indeed one to be carried out in collaboration with God; the Bible itself calls us to this. It does not imply, however, a historicization of God in the sense that Pixley seems to postulate. Furthermore, although Pixley is legitimately concerned that justice should be established within history, the perspective of contemplation and gratuitousness is, in my opinion, missing from his understanding of the Book of Job. And without this perspective the commitment to justice loses its proper setting and scope. Historically, moreover, commitments lacking this perspective have quickly suffered exhaustion. This is the point I have been trying to bring out in these pages; I have been inspired to do so by, among other things, the book I am here criticizing.

24. "Gastar la vida," in *Oraciones a quemarropa* (Lima: CEP, 1982), p. 69. S. Kierkegaard writes: "In the whole Old Testament there is no other figure one approaches with so much human confidence, boldness and trust as Job, simply because he is so human in every way, because he resides in a *confinium* touching on poetry" (*Kierkegaard's Works,* Vol. VI, p. 204).

CONCLUSION

1. R. de Pury, *Job ou l'homme revolté,* cited by Barth, *Church Dogmatics,* IV/3, part 1, p. 424: "The remarkable thing about this Book is that Job makes not a single step of flight to a better God, but stays resolutely in the field of battle under the fire of the divine wrath. Although God treats him as an enemy, through the dark night and the abyss Job does not falter, nor invoke another court, nor even appeal to the God of his friends, but calls upon this God who crushes him. He flees to the God whom he accuses. He sets his confidence in God who has disillusioned him and reduced him to despair. . . . Without deviating from the violent assertion of his innocence and God's hostility, he confesses his hope, taking as his Defender the One who judges him, as his Liberator the One who throws him in prison, and as his Friend his mortal enemy."

2. See W. A. M. Beuker, "Mispat. The First Servant Song and Its Context," *Vetus Testamentum,* 22 (1972) 1–30.

3. Those who follow this road may draw encouragement from the words of St. Augustine to his people: "Therefore, brothers and sisters, let us now sing, not in the delight of repose but to ease our toil. As travelers are accustomed to sing, so do you sing but journey on; comfort yourself in your toil by singing. . . . If you advance, you are continuing your journey, but advance in goodness, in true faith, in good practices; sing and journey on" (*Sermon* 256, 1, 2–3 = PL 38:1193).

4. Despite reductionist interpretations that try to deny the fact, this conviction has been part of the theology of liberation from the beginning and has always fed the spirituality that animates this theology. The theme of the gratuitousness of divine love is therefore the point of reference for determining the ultimate meaning of the emphasis on the practice of justice; see my *A Theology of Liberation,* passim, and *We Drink from Our Own Wells,* pp. 117–26.

5. See A. Heschel, *The Prophets* (New York: Harper & Row, 1962), p. 201: "Justice dies when dehumanized. . . . Justice dies when deified, for beyond all justice is God's compasssion. The logic of justice may seem impersonal, yet the concern for justice is an act of love."

6. See John Paul II, encyclical *Rich in Mercy,* §7: "This redemption is the final, definitive revelation of the holiness of God who in His very being is the absolute fullness of perfection. This means that He is the fullness of justice and love, for justice is based on love, flows from it and seeks it as its crown" (*The Pope Speaks,* 26 [1981] 36–37). See also §14.

7. See J. M. González Ruíz, *Dios es gratuito, no superfluo* (Madrid/Barcelona: Marova/Fontanella, 1970).

8. The Puebla document is translated in *Puebla and Beyond: Documentation and Commentary,* J. Eagleson and P. Scharper, eds. (Maryknoll, N.Y.: Orbis Books, 1979). See H. Bourgeois, *Dieu selon les chrétiens* (Paris: Centurion, 1974), p. 58: "God is for him [Jesus] the generosity behind his own generosity. He is the primal source of the potentialities that Jesus finds in himself and elicits in those around him. God is here not an explanation but a permanent condition; a symbol for the symbolism of the human being; an image of the total gratuitousness that makes possible the limited and yet indefinitely extended gratuitousness of the human person."

9. J. J. González Faus observes in his *La Humanidad Nueva* (Madrid, 1975), that "these words—the only ones in which Jesus does not address God as *Abba*—reveal the deepest dimension of this death: . . . the dimension of abandonment by God" (2:131).

10. See J. Delorme, *Lecture de l'Evangile selon Saint Marc* (Paris: Cerf, 1972), p. 112: "It is clear that although Jesus recites only the opening words of Ps. 22, the reader is to know that the entire psalm is the key to an understanding of the crucifixion. The reader knows therefore that the attitude of Jesus during this time is that expressed in the prayer of the suffering just man, according to which the ill-treatment he suffers is the condition for a rebirth and for the success of God's plan (see Ps. 22:23–31)."

11. The meaning and historical character of these final moments of Jesus have been the subject of recent studies. See in particular the fresh and penetrating observations of X. Léon-Dufour, *Face à la mort: Jésus et Paul* (Paris: Seuil, 1979), esp. pp. 149–67.

12. See Walter Kasper, *Jesus the Christ* (New York: Paulist, 1976), p. 118: "This psalm [22] is a lament which turns into a song of thanksgiving. The religious man's suffering is experienced as abandonment by God; but in his suffering and in the agony of death the religious man finds that God has been Lord all along, and that he saves him

and brings him into a new life. The psalm uses the language of apocalyptic to put this experience into the form of a typical, paradigmatic fate. Being saved from death now becomes the way in which the eschatological kingdom of God intervenes. Consequently Jesus' words, 'My God, my God, why hast thou forsaken me?' are not a cry of despair but a prayer confident of an answer; and one which hopes for the coming of God's kingdom."

13. See Ingrid González, "Salmos de lamentación: Protesta ante el sufrimiento," *Vida y Pensamiento* (San José, Costa Rica), 4/1–2 (1984) 69–88. At the end of her essay the author reproduces the free translations, inspired by the situation in Latin America, that Ernesto Cardenal, Mamerto Menapace, and she herself have made of Psalm 22.

14. This ("la miseria del misero") is how the *Biblia de Jerusalén* translates v. 25. [The French *Bible de Jérusalem* has "la pauvreté du pauvre," the *Jerusalem Bible* has "the poor man in his poverty," and the *New Jerusalem Bible* has "the poverty of the poor."—TR.]

15. See P. Beauchamp, *Psaumes nuit et jour* (Paris: Seuil, 1977), pp. 233–52.

16. J. Delorme (*Lecture*) links the final words of Jesus with Job: "The abandonment that Jesus experiences must be taken seriously, but it must be interpreted not according to our modern outlook that looks upon it as a cry of despair, but according to the biblical outlook for which the sense of abandonment is the occasion for a new outburst of faith: 'I have no hope; you, God, are my only hope, and you are abandoning me. Only you can explain to me why I am in this situation; therefore I shall keep after you until you do explain it. Meanwhile I put myself in your hands no matter what happens.' Neither was the cry of Job a cry of despair: if he keeps pressing heaven with his questions, it is simply because he expects God to answer. He lays on God the obligation of answering, and not only at this moment; until he dies he will go on demanding justice (Job 19:25–27). His is the cry of a madman, for it expresses a hope his age found inconceivable. But thanks to this faith that perseveres to the end, his cry is, as it were, the revelation of a step forward" (pp. 112–13).

17. Léon-Dufour, *Face à la mort*, p. 164: "The Markan and Lukan traditions both make use of the 'lamentation' pattern. . . . They have selected from these prayers of suffering and trust [Psalms 22 and 31] the words that can best serve as point of departure for a positive response from God. According to Mark, Jesus makes his own the sentiments of the suffering just man: behind his words we can hear the cry of the persecuted but trusting just man. The same holds for Luke, but with a quite different tonality and with the appeal to the 'Father.' "

18. This is clearly pointed out in the final report of the 1985 Synod of Bishops, which had been convoked to review the implementation of Vatican II over a period of twenty years. In Section D 2 the report reads: "It seems to us that in the present-day difficulties God wishes to teach us more deeply the value, the importance, and the centrality of the cross of Jesus Christ. Therefore the relationship between human history and salvation history is to be explained in the light of the paschal mystery. Certainly the theology of the cross does not at all exclude the theology of the creation and incarnation, but, as is clear, it presupposes it. When we Christians speak of the cross, we do not deserve to be labeled pessimists, but we rather base ourselves upon the realism of Christian hope" (text printed in *East Asian Pastoral Review*, 23/1 [1986] 22).

19. Because of my theme I am especially concerned in these pages with the element of loneliness and communion in the cross and resurrection of Christ, to the extent that these have to do with talk about God. On the comprehensive meaning of the redemptive experience of Jesus, see C. Duquoc, *Christologie*, vol. 2, *Le Messie* (Paris: Cerf, 1972),

pp. 171–226; E. Schillebeeckx, *Jesus: An Experiment in Christology* (New York: Seabury, 1979), pp. 179–271.

20. L. Boff, "Como predicar la cruz hoy," *Christus* (Mexico City), 573–74 (March-April, 1984), 22, writes: "The supreme theological art is to be able to speak of death and the cross."

21. See J. B. Metz, "The Future in the Memory of Suffering," *Concilium,* 76 (1972) 9–25.

22. See G. Gutiérrez, *Beber en su propio pozo* (rev. and enlarged ed.; Lima: CEP, 1983), p. 204.

23. See J. Moltmann, *The Crucified God: The Cross of Christ as the Foundation and Criticism of Christian Theology* (New York: Harper & Row, 1974), p. 153: "Every theology that claims to be Christian must come to terms with Jesus' cry on the cross. Basically, every Christian theology is consciously or unconsciously answering the question, 'Why hast thou forsaken me?' . . . Sharing in the sufferings of this time, Christian theology is truly contemporary theology."

24. Pascal, *Pensées* (Baltimore: Penguin, 1968), no. 919 (p. 313).

25. I phrase my thought in this way because human suffering is not limited to suffering caused by social injustice. It is undeniable, however, that this latter kind of suffering is found on a vast scale and marked by refined cruelty in Latin America; that many other human wants have their origin in it; that it is occasioned by a contempt for the life of the poor that has its roots in sin—that is, in the refusal to love God and other human beings; and that the responsibility for removing its causes is ours, at least in part. Throughout these pages I have tried to keep in mind the complexity of human suffering.

26. In his essay "Facing the Jews: Christian Theology after Auschwitz," *Concilium,* 175 (1984) 26, Metz writes: "Søren Kierkegaard: In order to experience and understand what it means to be a Christian, it is always necessary to recognize a definitive historical situation. I start with the idea that Kierkegaard is right (without being able to explain this in detail at this time). The situation without the recognition of which Christian theology does not know whereof it speaks, is for us in this country first of all 'after Auschwitz.'" Some years before, Metz had sketched the problem in an article entitled "Christians and Jews after Auschwitz," which was reprinted in *Beyond Civic Religion* (Mainz/Munich, 1980), pp. 29–50. There the author points out the historical responsibility of Christians for Auschwitz. They have the same responsibility for the situation that Latin America is experiencing and to which I refer in what follows.

27. R. Rubinstein, *The Religious Imagination: A Study in Psychoanalysis and Jewish Theology* (Indianapolis: Bobbs-Merrill, 1968), and A. Neher, *L'exil de la parole: Du silence biblique au silence d'Auschwitz* (Paris: Seuil, 1970), have strongly emphasized this absence of God and related it to the experience of Job. See the excellent review of these two books by P. Watte, "Job à Auschwitz," *Revue théologique de Louvain,* 4 (1973) 173–90.

28. I am thinking of Central America in particular. In this context, see the testimonies given by the tenacious and heroic people of Nicaragua in T. Cabestrero, *Nicaragua: crónica de una sangre inocente* (Mexico City: Katun, 1985); Engl. trans., *Blood of the Innocent* (Maryknoll, N.Y.: Orbis Books, 1985).

29. This is the meaning of the Quechuan word "Ayacucho."

30. "Holy Father, we are hungry, we suffer affliction, we lack work, we are sick. Our hearts are crushed by suffering as we see our tubercular wives giving birth, our children dying, our sons and daughters growing up weak and without a future. Yet despite everything we believe in the God of life." These were the words with which Víctor and

Isabel Chero greeted John Paul II when he visited one of the poorest areas of Lima. In a strongly worded, improvised response, the pope repeated what the inhabitants had said about their hunger for bread and their hunger for God. See the texts in "Villa El Salvador: un diálogo del Papa con los pobres," *Páginas,* 68 (April 1985) 34–37.

31. From the words of the cantata "Santa María de Iquique" by Claudio Sapian, cited in J. Míguez Bonino, "Compromiso cristiano ante el sufrimiento," *Christus* (Mexico City), 573–74 (March-April 1984) 35–41; the author has some excellent reflections on the theme.

32. Alonso Schökel (*Job* [chap. 1, n. 1, above]) says forcefully and aptly: "God did not shut Job's mouth as soon as he ended his opening curse (chap. 3). God does not look for mute co-workers; God wants the words of Job. Because we, though a critical people, critical even of God, lack our own words, Job is our spokesman. That is why he could not keep quiet. Beyond our criticisms of the God whom our critical minds invent, comes the voice of the ever true God. Job could not keep quiet" (p. 597).

33. The Apocalypse has the Lamb drying the tears of those who have come out of the great tribulation (Rev. 7:17).

34. See the remarks on Luke 10 in G. Gutiérrez, *A Theology of Liberation* (Maryknoll, N.Y.: Orbis, 1973), pp. 198–200.

35. See Jon Sobrino, *Christology at the Crossroads: A Latin American Approach* (Maryknoll, N.Y.: Orbis, 1978), p. 231: "There is the abandonment by God that Jesus felt on the cross and the abandonment by God that we experience. There is the cry of Jesus on the cross and the cry of countless victims in history. They do not allow us to nurture an ingenuous faith in God; it must be a faith that overcomes the world (1 John 5:4)."

36. Cited in Léon-Dufour, *Face à la mort,* p. 167.

Scripture Index

A THEOLOGY OF LIBERATION
by Gustavo Gutiérrez
One of the classics of liberation theology now in its tenth printing.

"This book must be read, not once but several times, by those who are interested in doing theology today." *Commonweal*

"This is one of the most acute and the most readable theological essays of today on the meaning and mission of the Church." *Catholic Library World*

no. 478-X **334pp. pbk.**

THE POWER OF THE POOR IN HISTORY
by Gustavo Gutiérrez
Eight major essays that examine developments in liberation theology since Medellín with a focus on the option for the poor and the historical role of the poor in the liberation process.

"Gutiérrez is the first person in modern history to reactualize the great Christian themes of theology starting from a fundamental option for the poor. . . ." *Edward Schillebeeckx*

no. 388-0 **256pp. pbk.**

WE DRINK FROM OUR OWN WELLS
The Spiritual Journey of a People
by Gustavo Gutiérrez
"Gustavo Gutiérrez develops a spirituality which grows out of the lived experience of the Latin American people. Rooted in the reality of oppression and repression, this book calls forth a conversion from self-complacency and self sufficiency to that of solidarity with the poor." *Catholic New Times*

". . . it powerfully and beautifully provides a guide for 'the spiritual journey of a people,' a people of whom we too are a part." *Robert McAfee Brown*

no. 707-X **176pp. pbk.**

BIBLE OF THE OPPRESSED
by Elsa Tamez
Elsa Tamez, professor of biblical studies in San José, Costa Rica, examines nine Hebrew words for oppression in the Old Testament and in each case asks: what understanding of oppression is conveyed by the word, who are the agents of oppression, who are the

objects, and what are the methods used to oppress? She relates the biblical story of oppression and liberation to the contemporary Latin American scene.

no. 035-0   88pp. pbk.

GOD SO LOVED THE THIRD WORLD
The Bible, the Reformation, and Liberation Theologies
by Thomas D. Hanks

From an evangelical perspective, Thomas Hanks offers a thorough, biblical study of poverty and oppression and applies his findings to Latin America.

"This challenging and compelling work adds another special interest to biblical scholars, theologians, church people, and even Latin American scholars."   *Choice*

no. 152-7   176pp. pbk.

EXODUS
A Hermeneutics of Freedom
by J. Severino Croatto

Against the background of liberation theology, Severino Croatto shows how the kerygma of liberation is treated as a theme in the Bible in order to "orchestrate a method for rereading the Bible from the standpoint of the situation in Latin America."

"This is a challenging book. It challenges us to rethink our position on interpreting the text, and to regard ourselves as also bound up with the situation in Latin America."

Emmanuel

no. 111-X   96pp. pbk.

GOD OF THE LOWLY
Socio-Historical Interpretations of the Bible
Willy Schottroff and Wolfgang Stegemann, Eds.
trans. by Matthew J. O'Connell

A German theological best-seller now available in translation from Orbis. Stegemann, Solle, Luise and Willy Schottroff, and other members of the rising "materialist school" of biblical interpretation in Europe elaborate their method and expose the Bible's partiality for the weak, the underprivileged, and the poor.

"These essays combine the expected German thoroughness in critical exegesis with an acute analysis of social context to build 'a bridge of love' between our world and the biblical world. This is an important contribution to a liberating knowledge of scripture."

Norman K. Gottwald

no. 153-5   176pp. pbk.